BURTON MORRIS

POP!

BURTON MORRIS

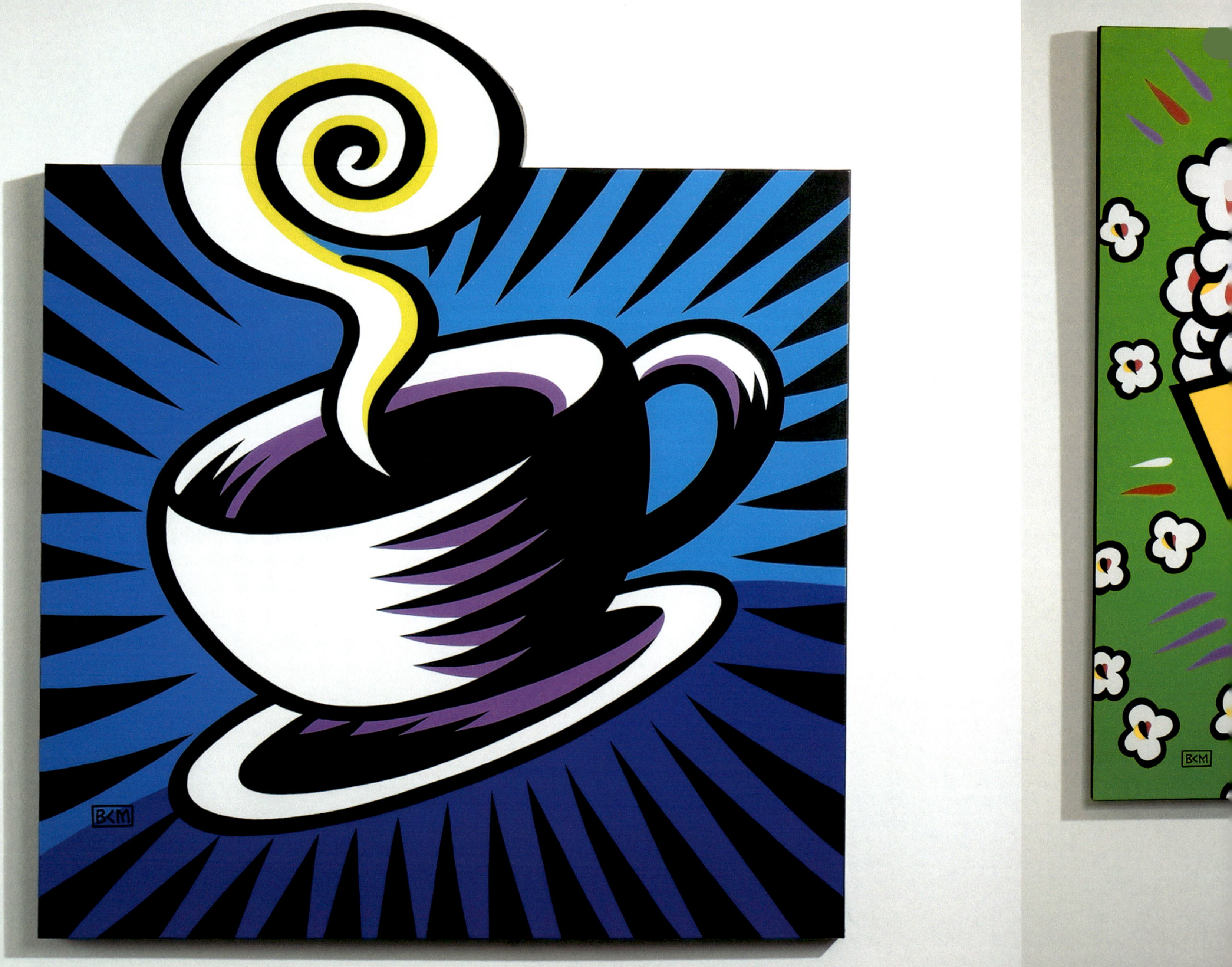

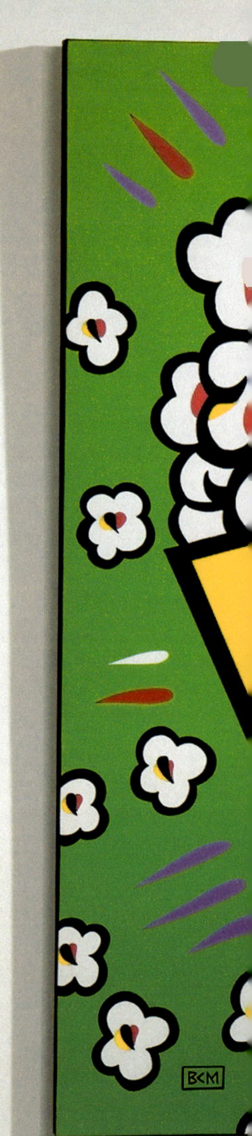

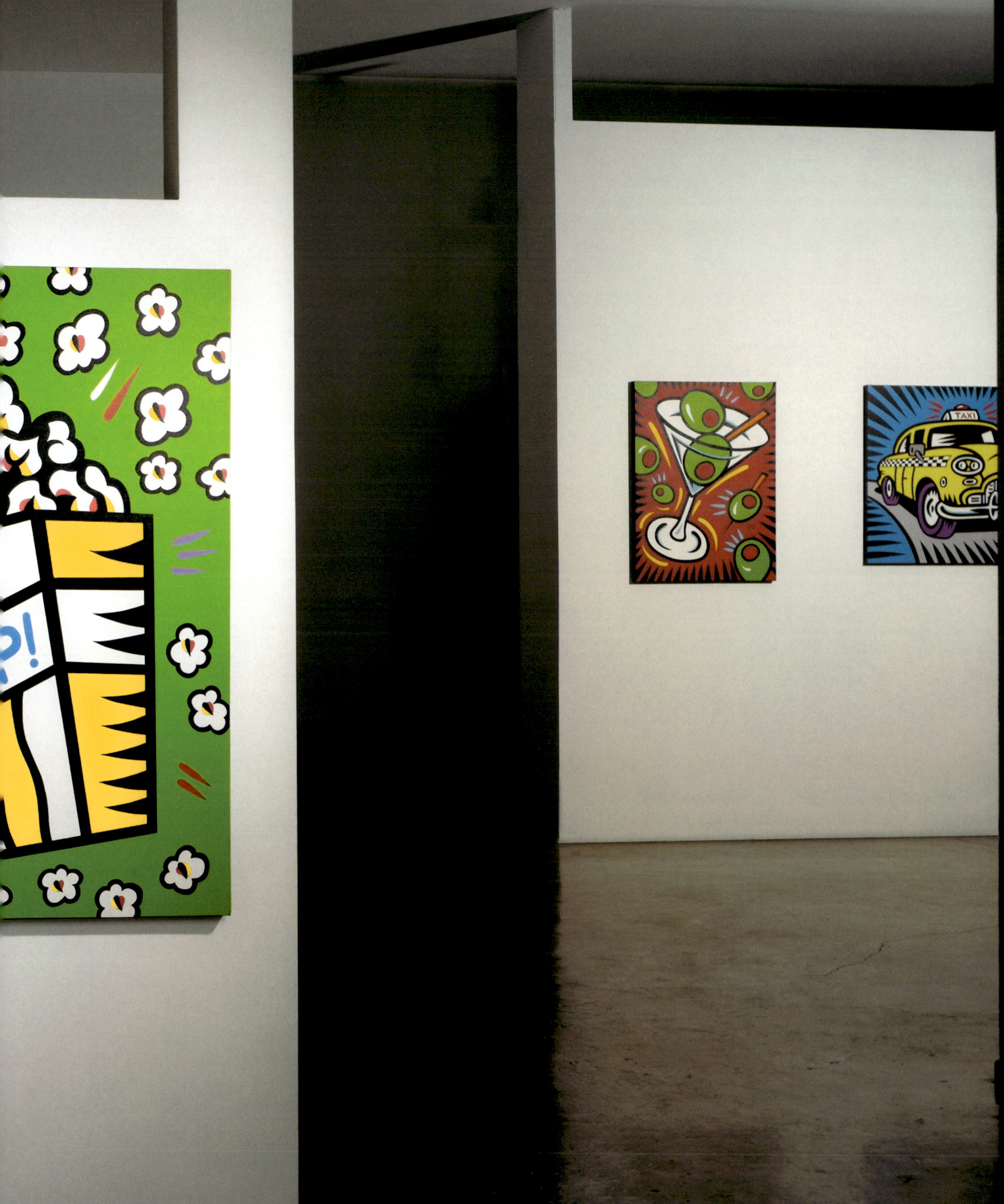

TAXI

PUBLISHERS: Alan Smith and Burton Morris
DESIGN AND ART DIRECTION: Felix Haro
DESIGN CONSULTANT: Monte Beauchamp
PRINTING: RR Donnelley, Hoechstetter Plant
PHOTO CREDITS: Jeff Sarpa and April Hubal
LIMITED EDITIONS: Screened Images Inc.

www.BurtonMorris.com

ISBN 978-0-615-15848-8

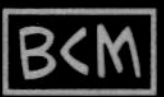

To SVETLANA ♡ & JARON & Marc,
5. 2011
Enjoy!

A FEW WORDS FROM THE ARTIST

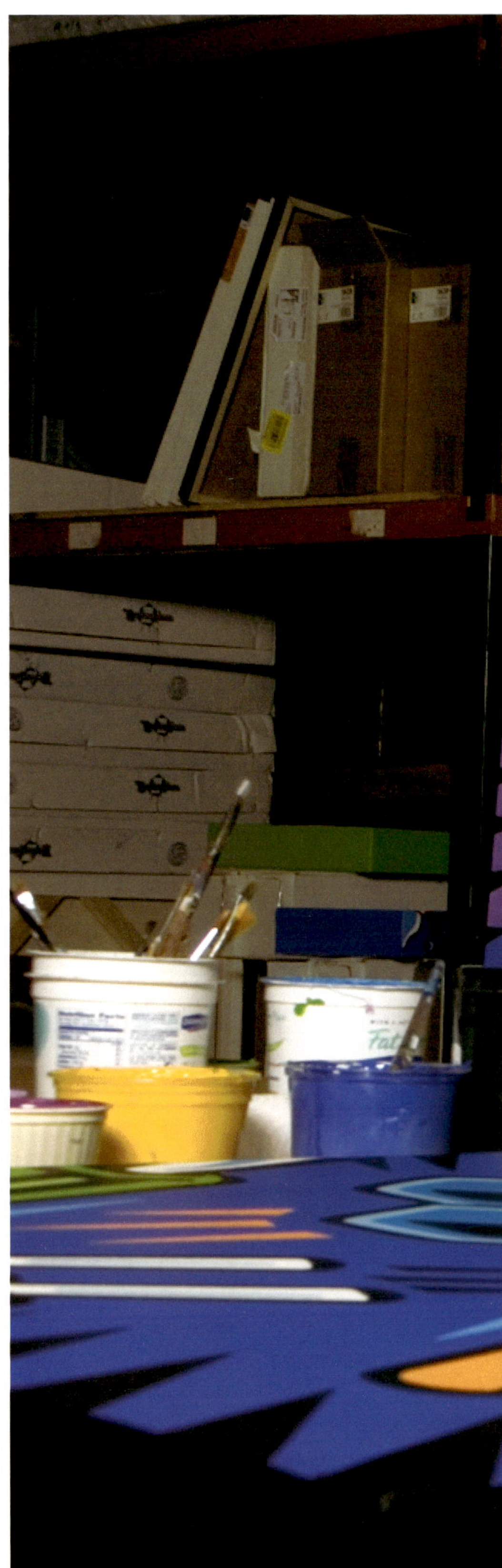

This book is an introduction to my artwork that showcases some of my favorite iconic images that I've created throughout the last two decades.

As a child, I was always attracted to the bright colors and energetic shapes of comic book art and cartoons. Everyday I would spend countless hours drawing, trying to teach myself about the fundamentals of art. My parents encouraged my talents and sent me to art classes close to our home at the Carnegie International Museum of Art in Pittsburgh, Pennsylvania. There, I was first exposed to great works of art from all over the world.

In my paintings, I try to create a universal appeal by taking objects and ideas and making them come to life. This creates art that is energetic, optimistic, and distinctive in style.

My career has taken me all over the world and has enabled me to expose my art to different cultures and to meet many fascinating people. I feel blessed everyday that I can live my life through art.

I'd like to thank everyone who has believed in my art and me over the years. Special thanks go to Stan Lee for his inspiration and encouraging words. My gratitude goes out to Donald Miller for his articulate insight into my work. I am deeply grateful to Thomas Sokolowski, Roy Disney, Andre Agassi, Bruce Davis, Donald Trump, Michele Roux, Francis Gabet and the late Fred Rogers, all of whom were generous enough to give me quotes for my book.

I am thankful to my parents, Marvin and Bunny, who encouraged me to pursue my dreams and taught me to believe in myself. I also wish to thank all of the galleries, collectors, teachers, staff, family and friends, who have supported me over the years. I am profoundly grateful to Alan Smith, whose loyalty, dedication, and hard work have helped guide my career. I dedicate this book to my beautiful wife, Sara, for being there by my side, and for all of her love and encouragement.

BURTON MORRIS

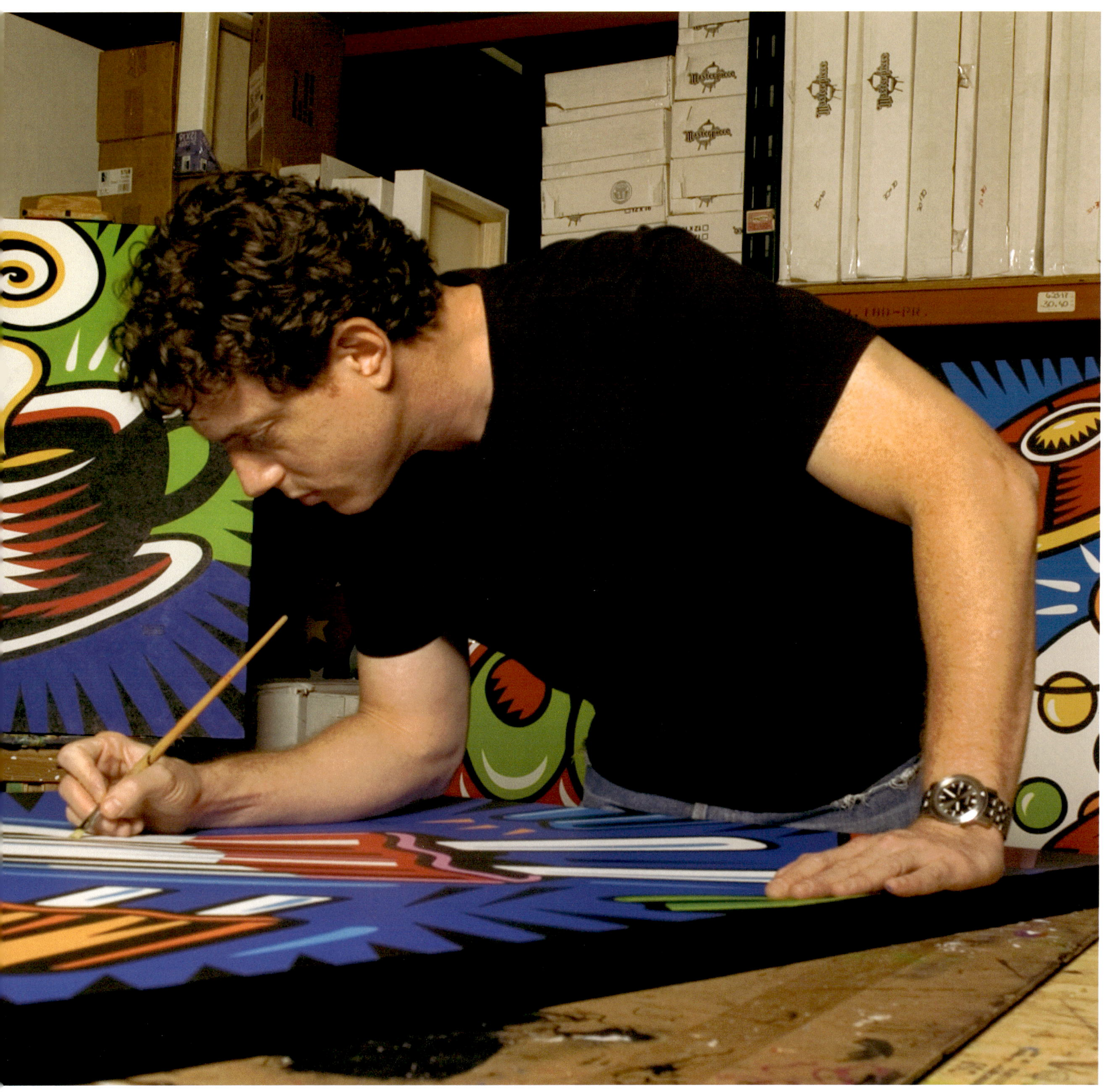

INTRODUCTION

by STAN LEE

Chief Creative Officer, POW Entertainment
Chairman Emeritus, Marvel Comics

POW!

As editor and art director of Marvel Comics, I've spent most of my adult life working with artists. So, when it comes to artwork, I felt I had seen it all.

But then I met Burton Morris! It happened not long ago when I was invited to sign autographs at a local Los Angeles book store. I had heard that an artist would also be there to exhibit his work but I didn't give that much thought.

Later, while I was signing, I could hear people in the store "oooh"ing and "ahhh"ing. Now I'll admit I'm a pretty good book signer, but there's nothing about my signature to cause such a reaction from the crowd. So I looked up to see what was happening.

That's when I got my first glimpse of Burton Morris' astonishing artwork. It was obvious why the fans were so impressed. Burton had a style so unique, so appealing and so totally crowd-pleasing that I had never seen anything like it.

The basic drawings, though simple, were cheerfulness personified. His use of color was incredibly daring, bright and sparkling. It is totally impossible to look at the art of Burton Morris without smiling. His are the most "feel good" paintings I have ever seen. Although beautifully crafted and superbly composed, Burton's style has a sophisticated simplicity which beggars description.

He has the uncanny ability to take the simplest object and, by his brilliant use of color and his incredible sense of design, make it seem as though one is seeing it and appreciating it for the first time.

Though Burton has been favorably compared to Andy Warhol and Roy Lichtenstein, his paintings have their own individuality, their own flavor and superb style that make them stand completely apart from the work of any other artist.

You can imagine how pleased I was when, upon meeting Burton, he told me he'd been a reader of my comics when he was young and had been greatly influenced by our superhero type artwork. In fact, he confessed he'd wanted to become a superhero artist but felt he couldn't quite do justice to that genre.

How very lucky for art lovers everywhere that Burton Morris abandoned his hope of drawing comic books and created his own style. No, even more than his own style—his own shining world, a world of painting like no other, a pop culture world of color and composition and cheer which he himself has created and which brings unimaginable joy to countless viewers around the globe.

I'm indescribably grateful for the opportunity to write these few words on Burton's behalf, for I think he is truly destined to rank with the great masters of art.

Finally, to me, the most exciting thing about Burton Morris is the fact that he's still a young man, driven by passion and blessed with energy. One can only imagine the new, fantastic paintings he'll continue to create in the years to come.

Excelsior!

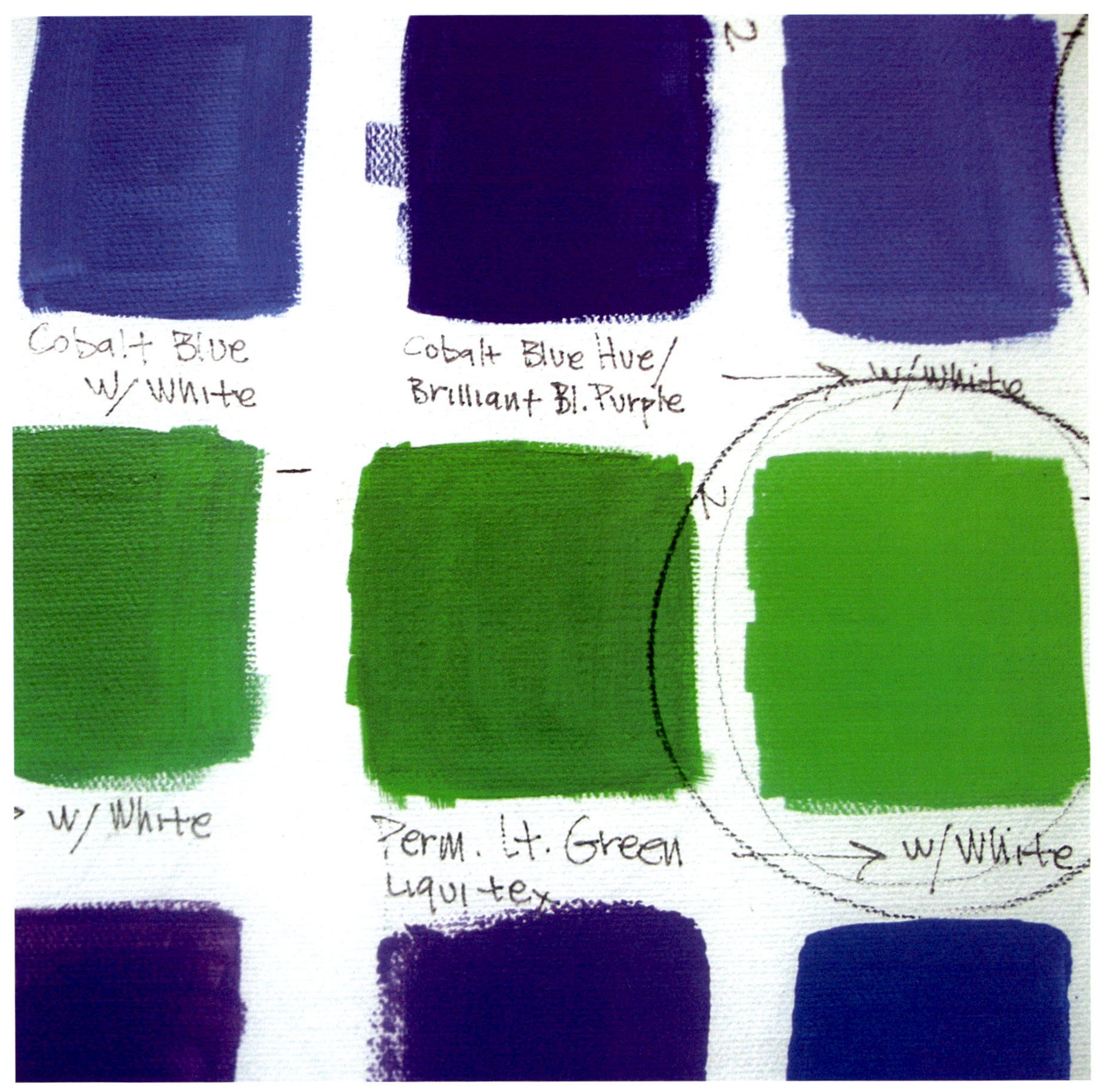

Cobalt Blue
w/ White
Cobalt Blue Hue/
Brilliant Bl. Purple
w/ White
w/ White
Perm. Lt. Green
Liquitex
w/ White

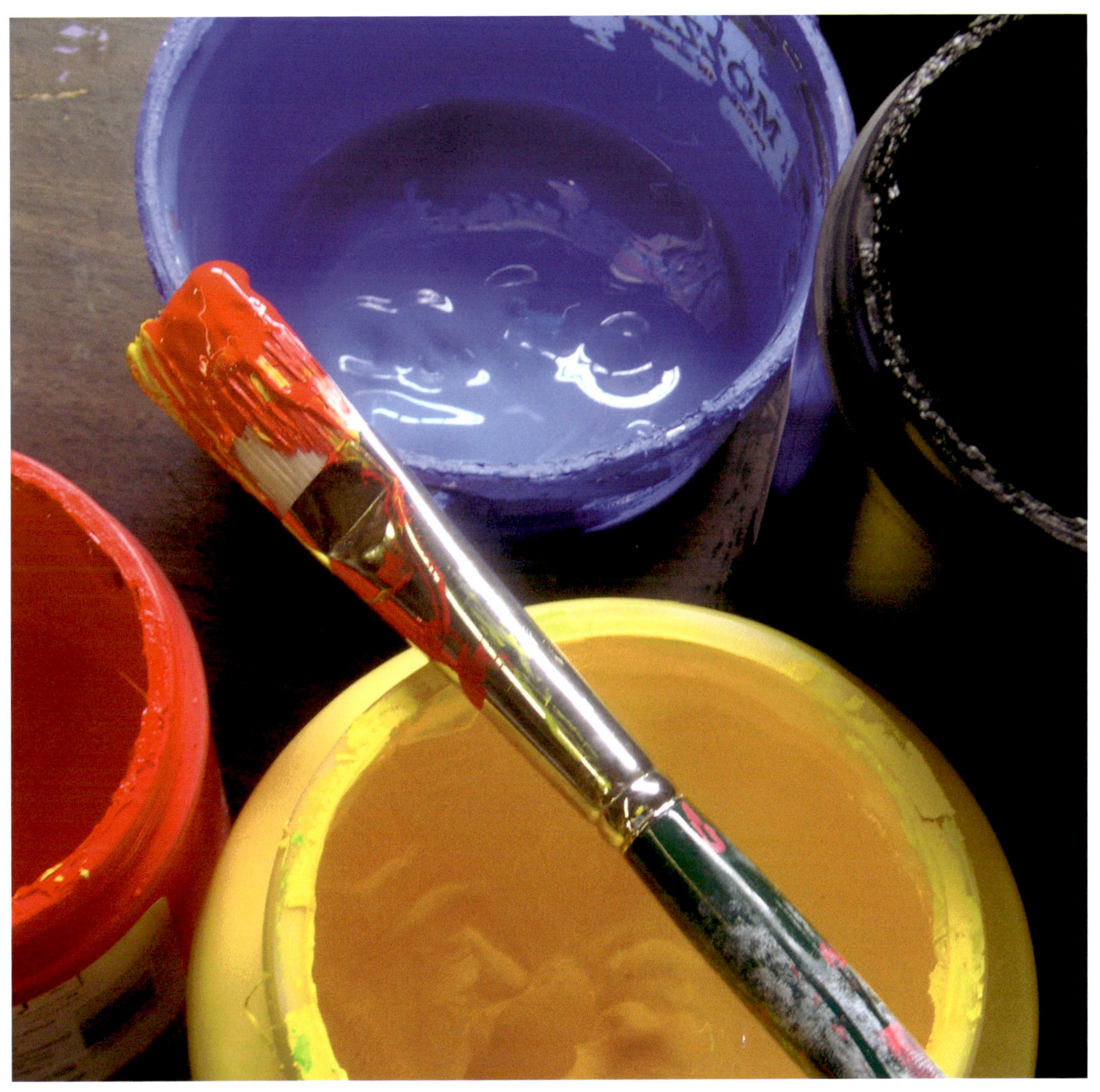

FOREWORD

by DONALD MILLER
Former Art and Architecture Critic
Pittsburgh Post Gazette

BURTON MORRIS' APPROACH TO FINE ART

Building on the legacy of Pop Art masters of the 1960s-70s, Burton Morris presents his personal world of popular American icons that put a delightful spin on everyday objects and motifs. In his post-Pop style, Morris boldly projects an enticing mood of happiness, high energy and fun. But his roots are in fine art.

Morris' forbears were icons Andy Warhol, Roy Lichtenstein, Tom Wesselmann and Red Grooms. He also employs some of the shorthand gestures of comic strips and magazines he has loved and emulated since childhood. These classic devices are seen in his simplified forms and action lines indicating movement joined with his rich acrylic colors. Morris imbues his art with his own impeccable style and optimistic frame of mind.

The artist's distinctive sword-like slashes suggesting shards of energy come from his study of woodcut prints. Two of his heroes are Albrecht Durer and Rockwell Kent. Durer used similar hatching in the sixteenth century. Twentieth century American artist Rockwell Kent illustrated books and designed bookplates with such lines. Artists for The New York Review of Books emulated his style in small India ink drawings, called "gloomies" in journalistic parlance.

Burton Morris was born in Pittsburgh, Pennsylvania in 1964. Like the late Pop artist Keith Haring, Morris felt an early attraction to Belgian artist Pierre Alechinsky's paintings that resemble fantastic comic strips. Both artists saw the Belgian's large exhibition in the International Series at the Carnegie Museum of Art, Pittsburgh, in 1977.

Morris earned his bachelor of fine arts degree at Carnegie Mellon University in 1986 and, during three more years while working at art directing and doing television commercials, he began developing his post-Pop drawings.

The artist established the Burton Morris Studios in 1990. That year he began making his small post-Pop icons more impressive by enlarging them. He also tightened his brushwork into his present precise style. He would choose one subject per composition to create what he calls "an instant happening" for the viewer.

Finding eager acceptance in the corporate world, Morris soon received commissions from Absolut Vodka, AT&T, Perrier, Microsoft, Sony and H.J. Heinz Corporation. He also began reaching out to a mass audience. For ten seasons, fans of the television sitcom Friends saw his work on the set.

Morris began expanding his artistic range with new conceptions. He worked beyond his pictures' edges and coordinated his images with three-dimensional objects made of painted wood that added intensity to his central images. He also created multi-panel paintings, often using such American icons as the Statue of Liberty and others in his bright and clean identifiable style.

In recent years Morris has exhibited his work in many venues. Among them are forty-two paintings and drawings shown at the renowned auction gallery Sotheby's branch in Amsterdam, the Netherlands. The International Olympic Committee selected the artist to produce thirty-six triumphant paintings on the spirit of the Olympic Games which exhibited at the International Olympic Museum in Lausanne, Switzerland, during the 2004 Summer Olympic Games in Athens, Greece.

Morris' work really burst onto the American stage and was given wide exposure in 2004 when he produced signature images for the 76th annual Academy Awards, perhaps best remembered for Morris' image of a young male photographer who faces forward with a light-exploding camera. Posters and banners with this icon enlivened the façade of the Kodak Theater and other sites in Hollywood and Los Angeles. The artist also produced art for the 38th Montreux Jazz Festival, the tenth annual Andre Agassi Charitable Foundation event and Major League Baseball's 2006 All-Star Game.

Morris has exhibited his eye-popping art in New York, Los Angeles, Miami, Boston, Pittsburgh as well as in Paris, Geneva, Hong Kong, Tokyo and Rome. His paintings are also part of many public and private collections.

But Burton Morris has only begun to show his considerable potential. He has proven he is alive to the world of large ideas. His talent, intensity, imagination and determination have always been present, and they continue to develop as he reaches his middle years. His talent reaches out boldly toward fresh artistic possibilities – whenever they occur, whatever they may be and wherever they take him.

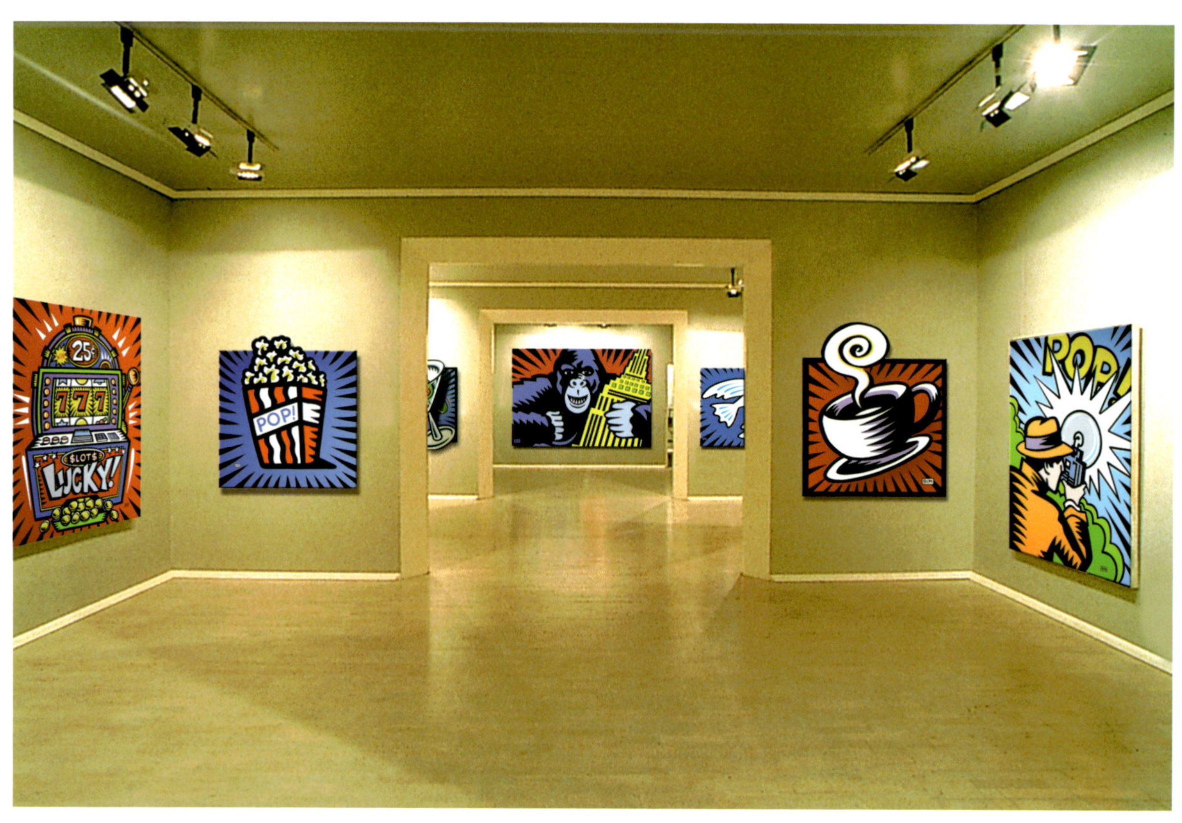

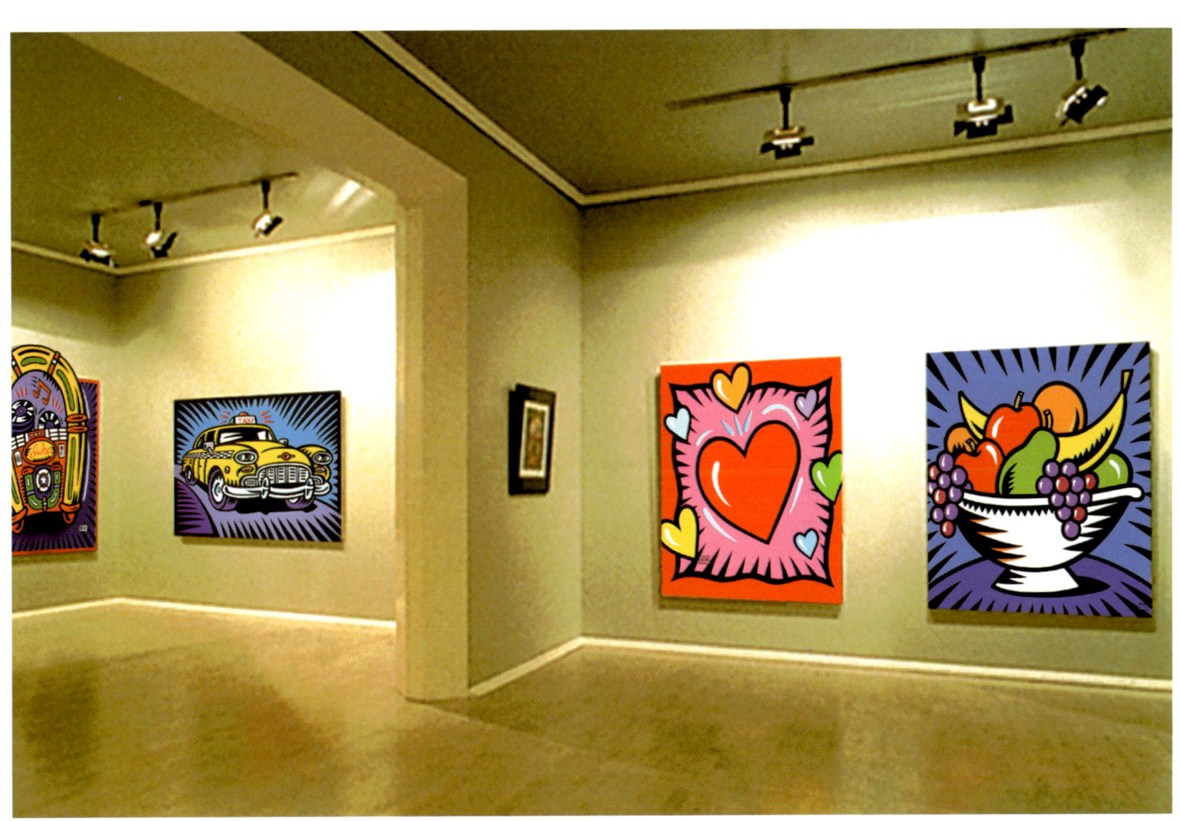

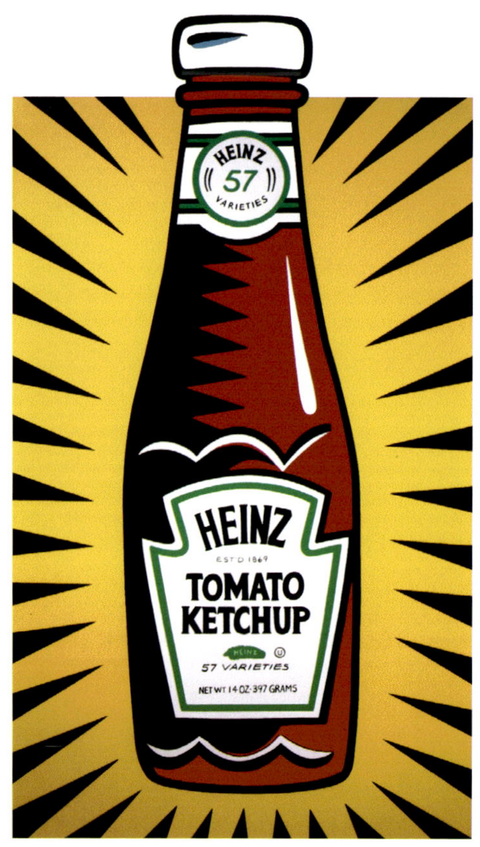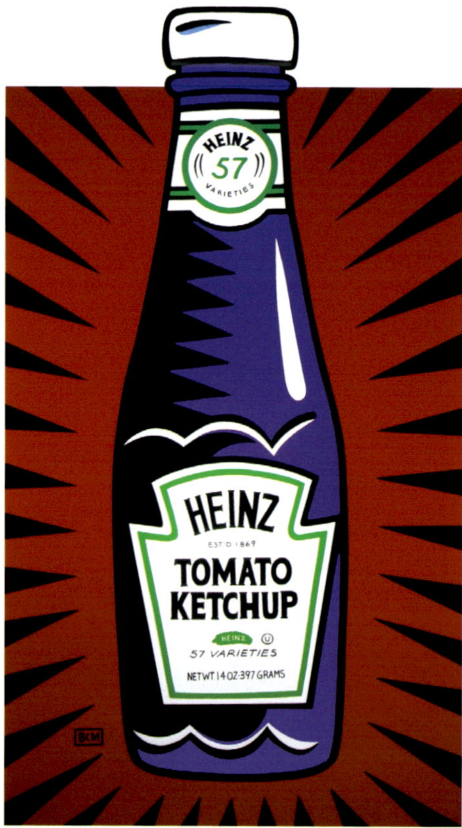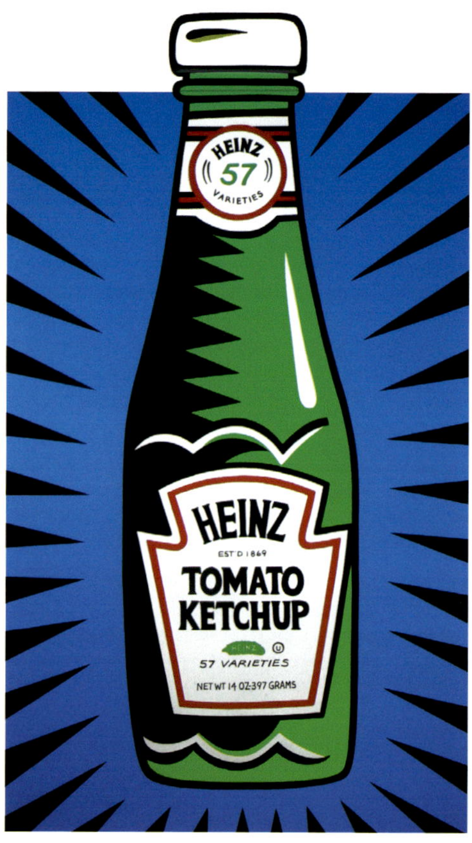

Heinz
2001
Acrylic paint on canvas
with hand cut wood extensions - triptych
50 x 36 inches
(127.0 x 91.44 cm)

"If Pop Art had a grandson,
it would surely be Burton Morris."

THOMAS SOKOLOWSKI
Director
The Andy Warhol Museum

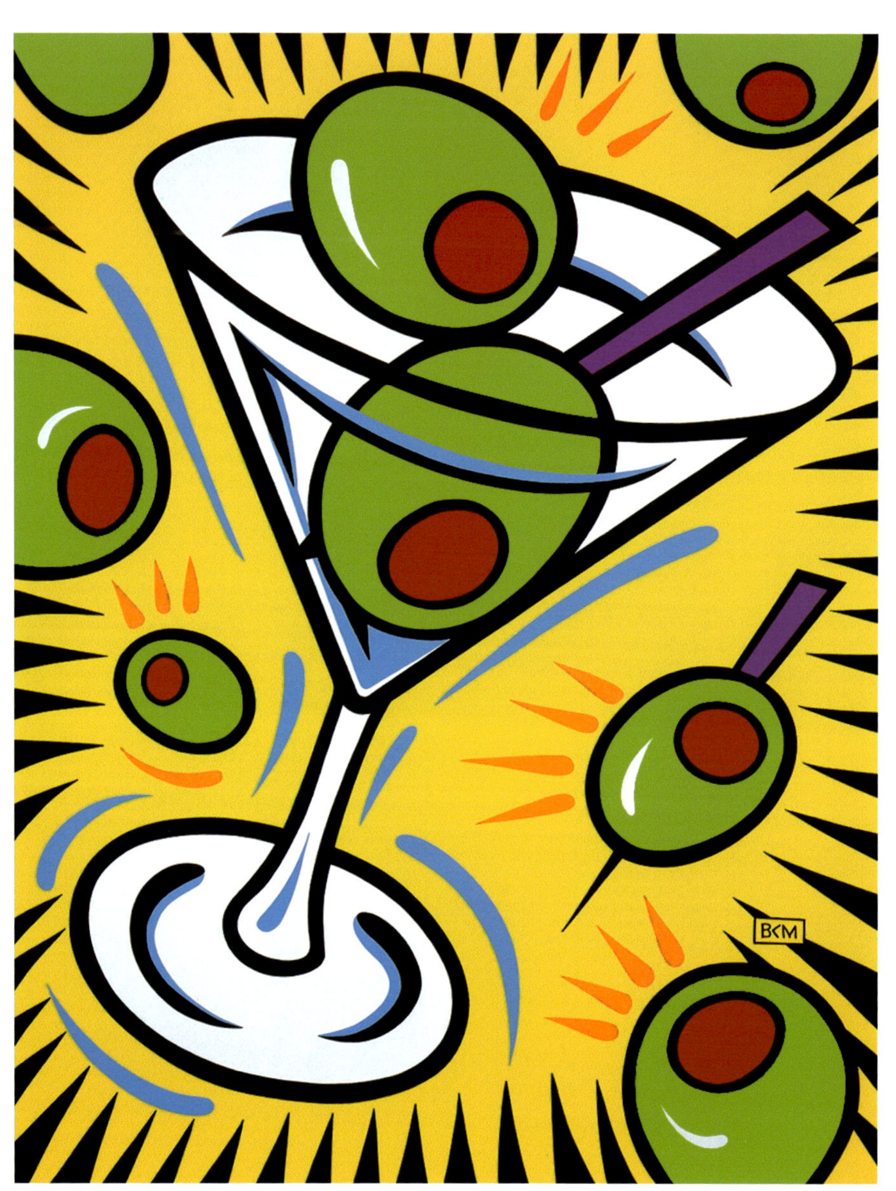

Shakin' Not Stirred
1998
Acrylic paint on canvas
48 x 36 inches
(121.92 x 91.44 cm)

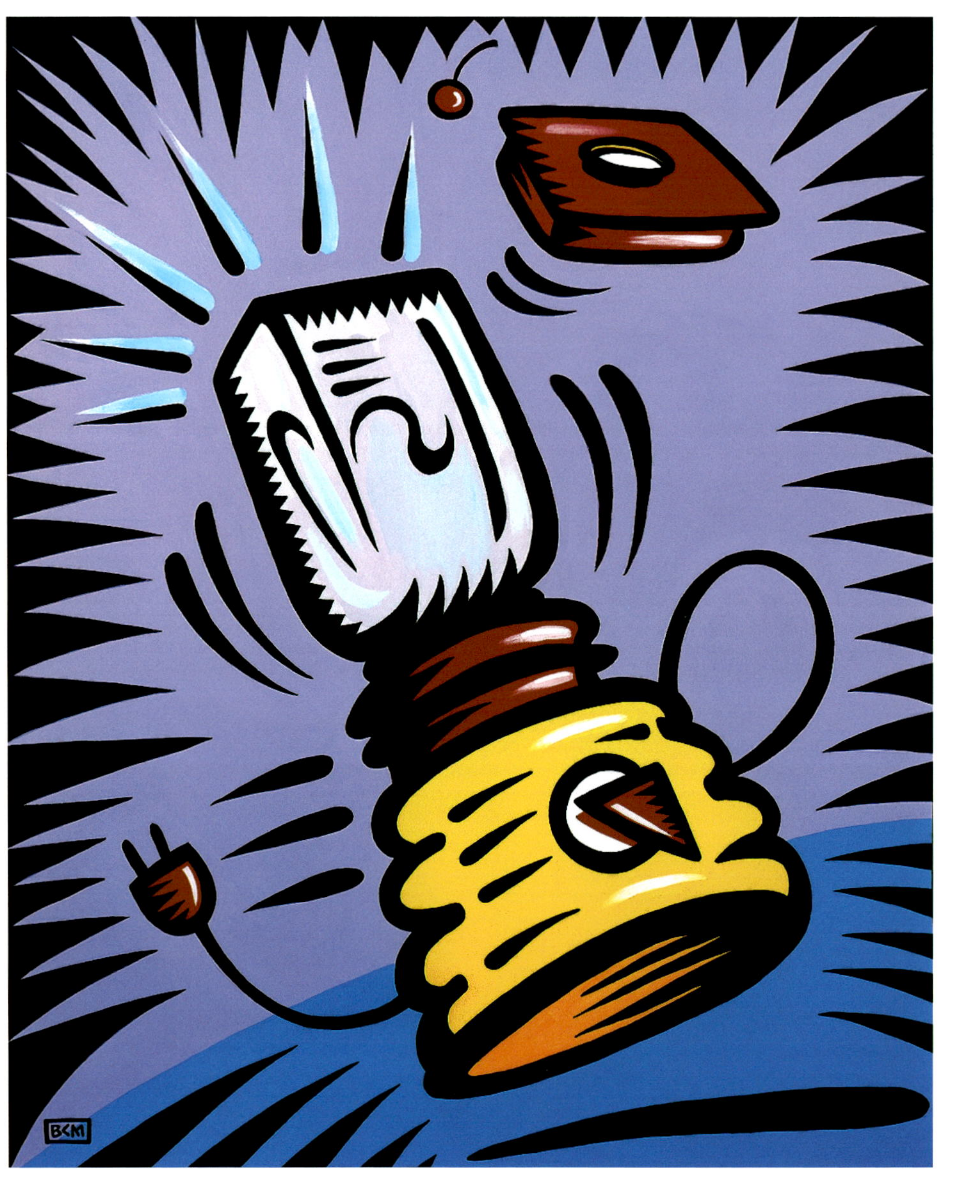

Cherry Delight
1994
Acrylic paint on canvas
60 x 48 inches
(152.4 x 121.92 cm)

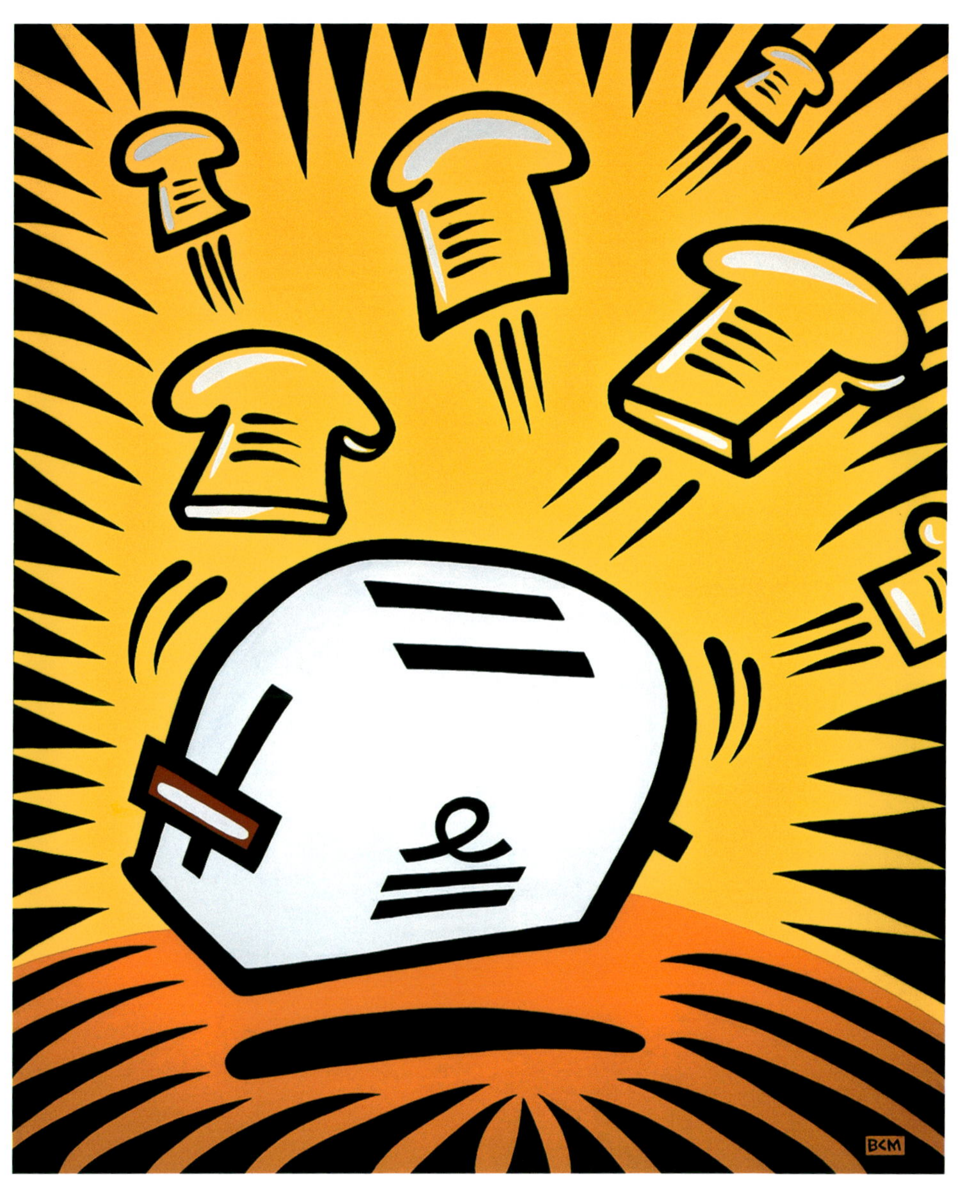

Jump Toast
1994
Acrylic paint on canvas
60 x 48 inches
(152.4 x 121.92 cm)

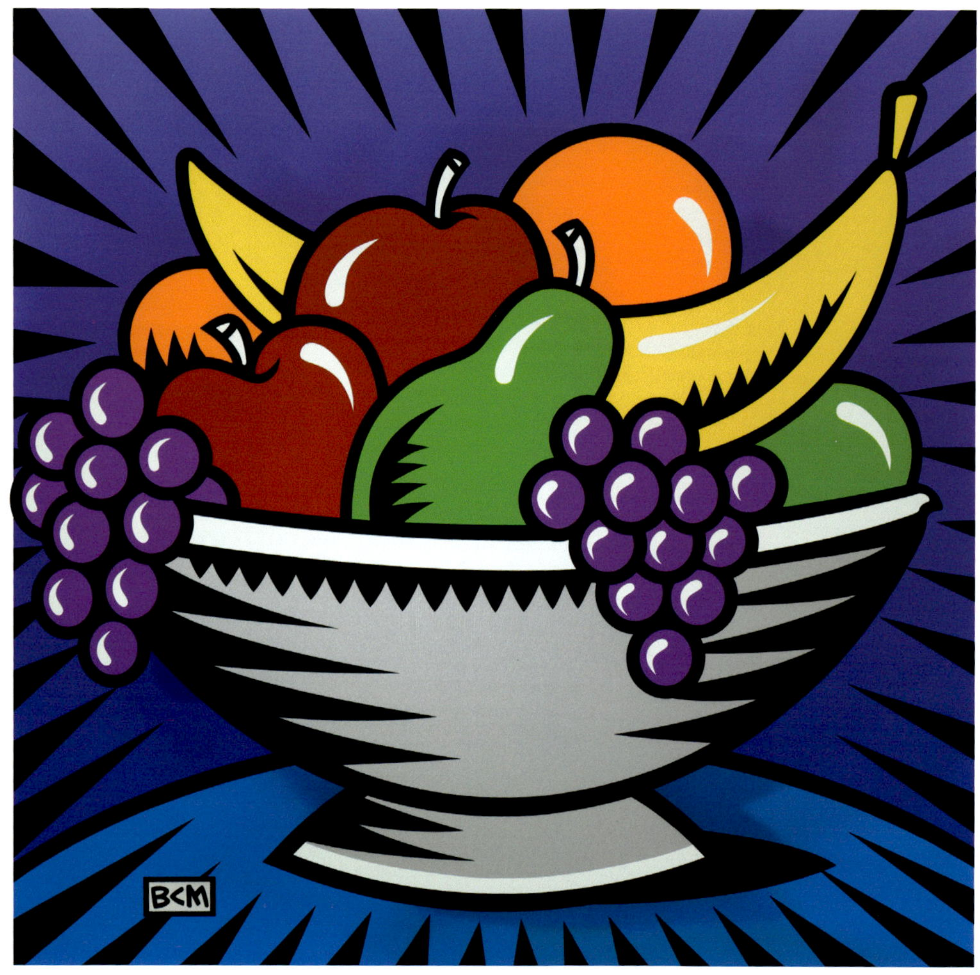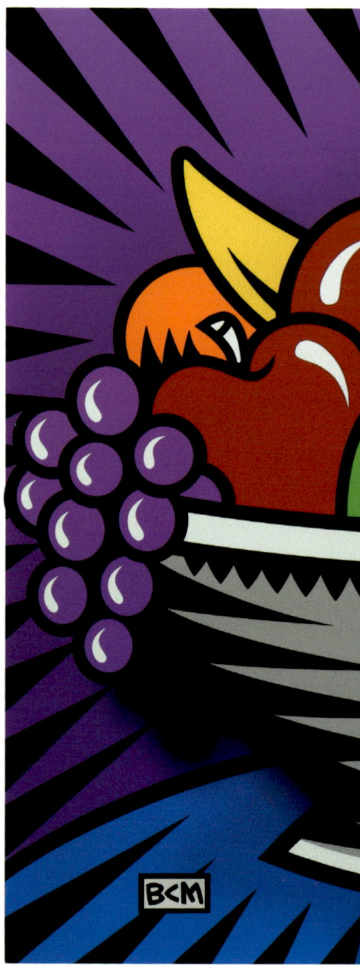

Fruitbowl (STILL LIFE)
2006
Silkscreen ink on gesso board
with dimensional pop–out front panel
Edition of 18
24 x 24 x 4 inches
(60.96 x 60.96 x 10.16 cm)

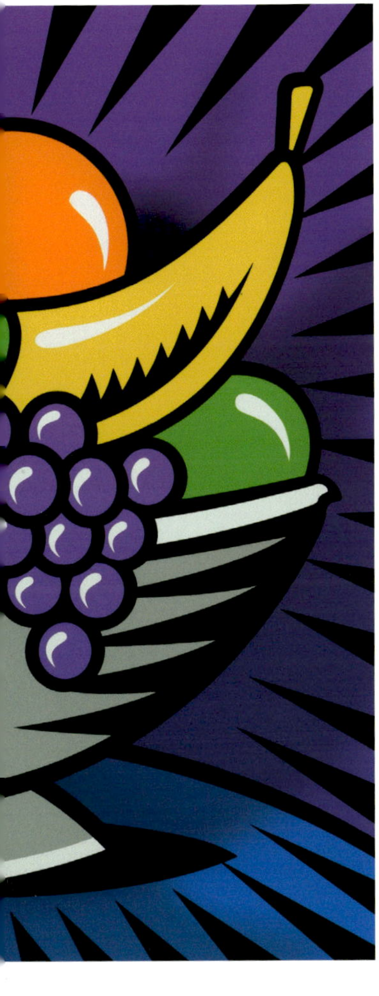
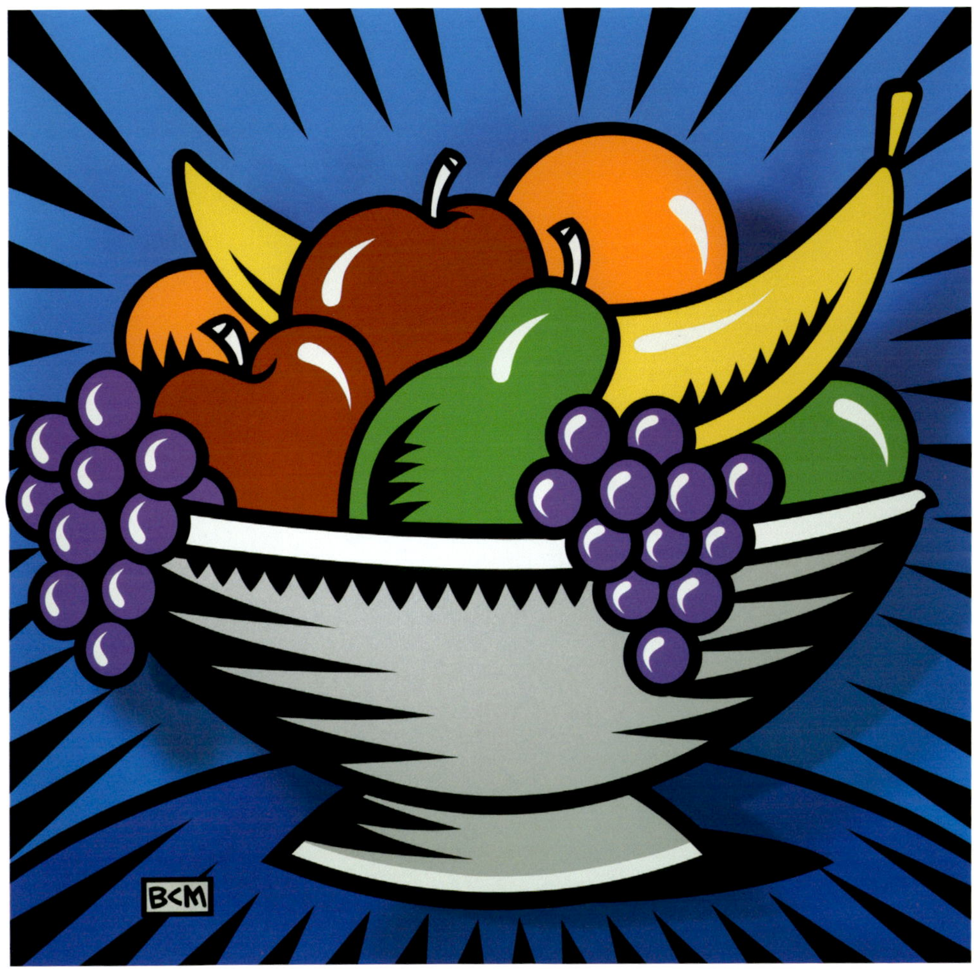

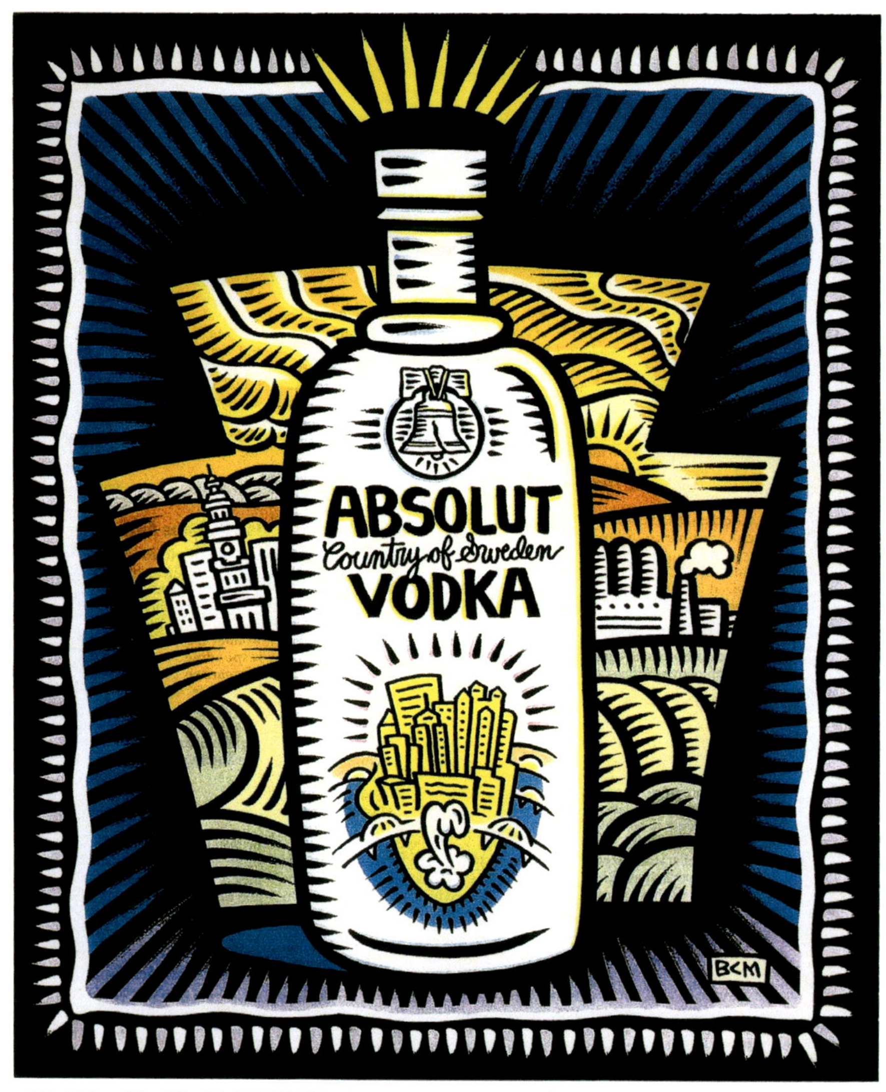

Absolut Pennsylvania
1993
Acrylic paint on canvas
(Advertisement from Absolut Statehood campaign)
60 x 48 inches
(152.4 x 121.92 cm)

"The work of Burton Morris has all the fresh and exciting qualities that make great Pop Art. In my experience dealing with many artists, I must say that Morris also has a great capacity for kindness. His personality is as magnanimous as his artwork is exceptional."

MICHEL P. ROUX
Chairman/C.E.O.
Crillon Importers LTD.

Coffee Cup
1997
Acrylic paint on canvas
with hand cut wood extension
42 x 36 inches
(106.68 x 91.44 cm)

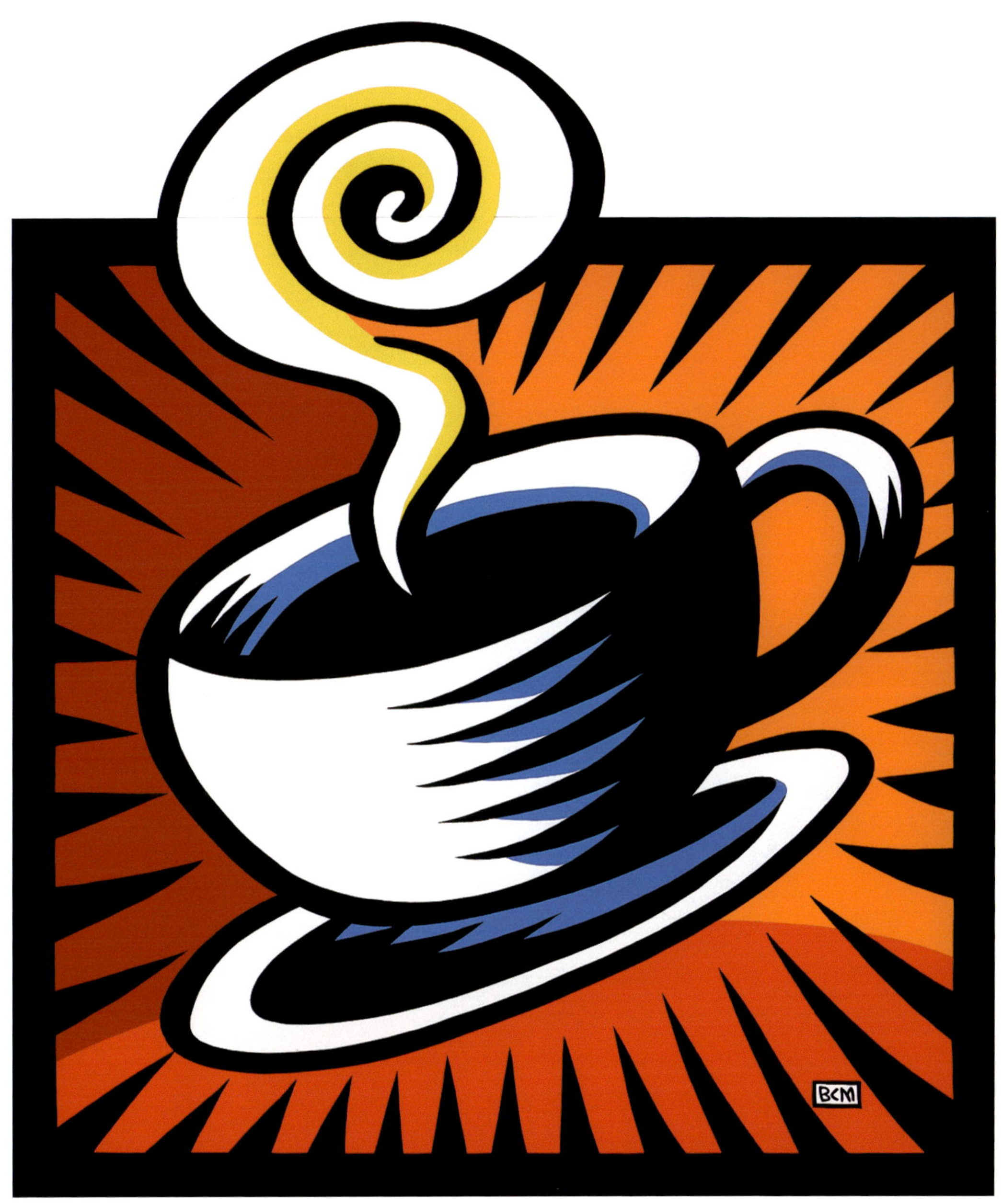

Popcorn
1999
Acrylic paint on wood
with hand cut dimensional pop-out front panel
28 x 24 x 3 inches
(71.12 x 60.96 x 7.62 cm)

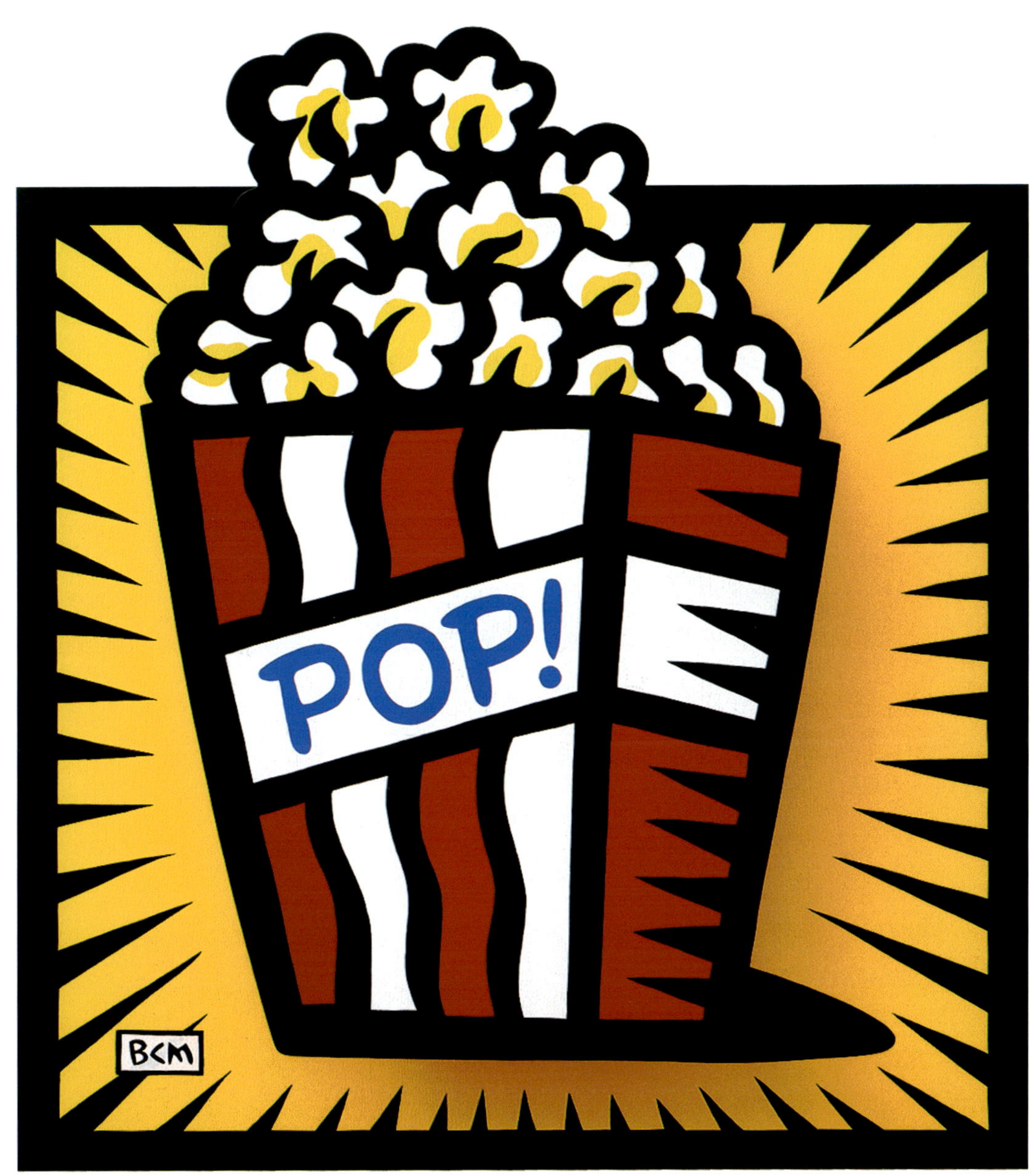

POP!
BCM

Lovebug
2002
Acrylic paint on canvas
36 x 48 inches
(91.44 x 121.92 cm)

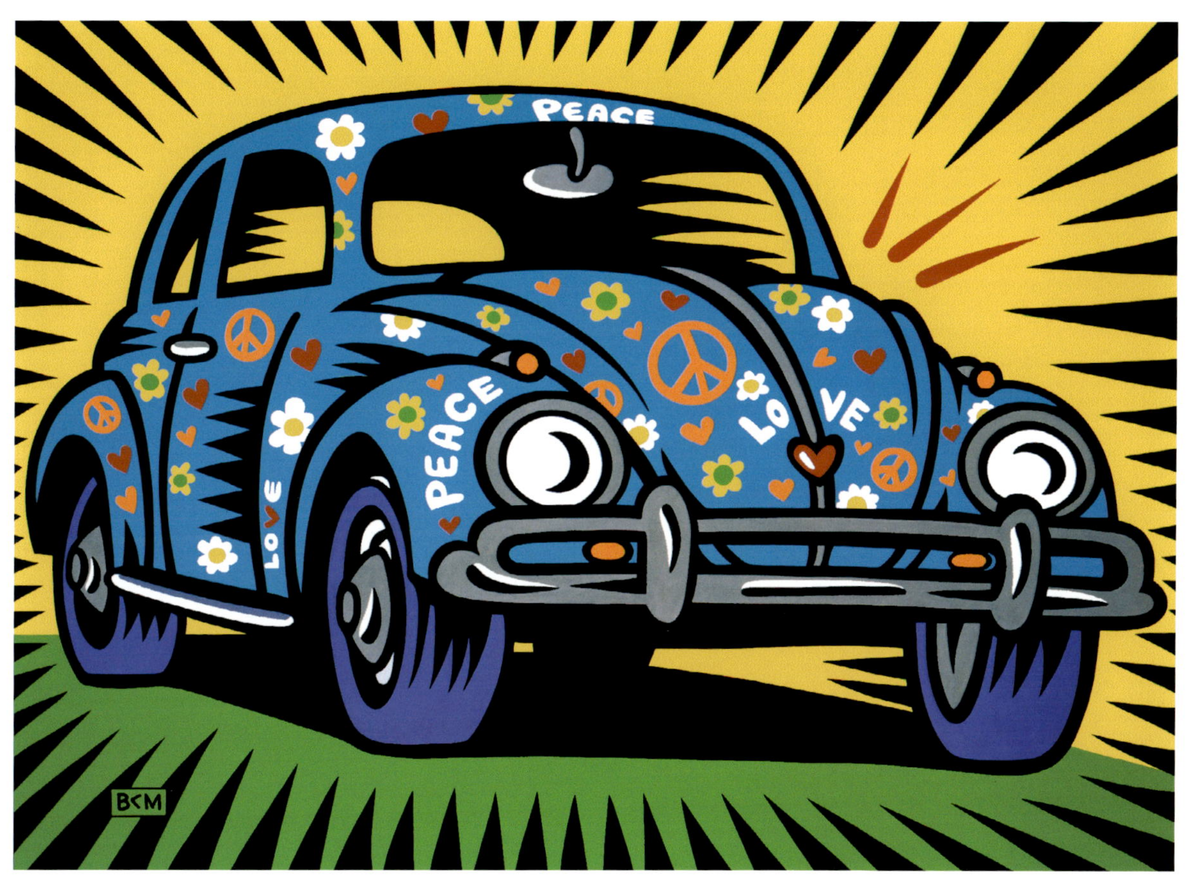

PEACE
PEACE
LOVE
LOVE
BCM

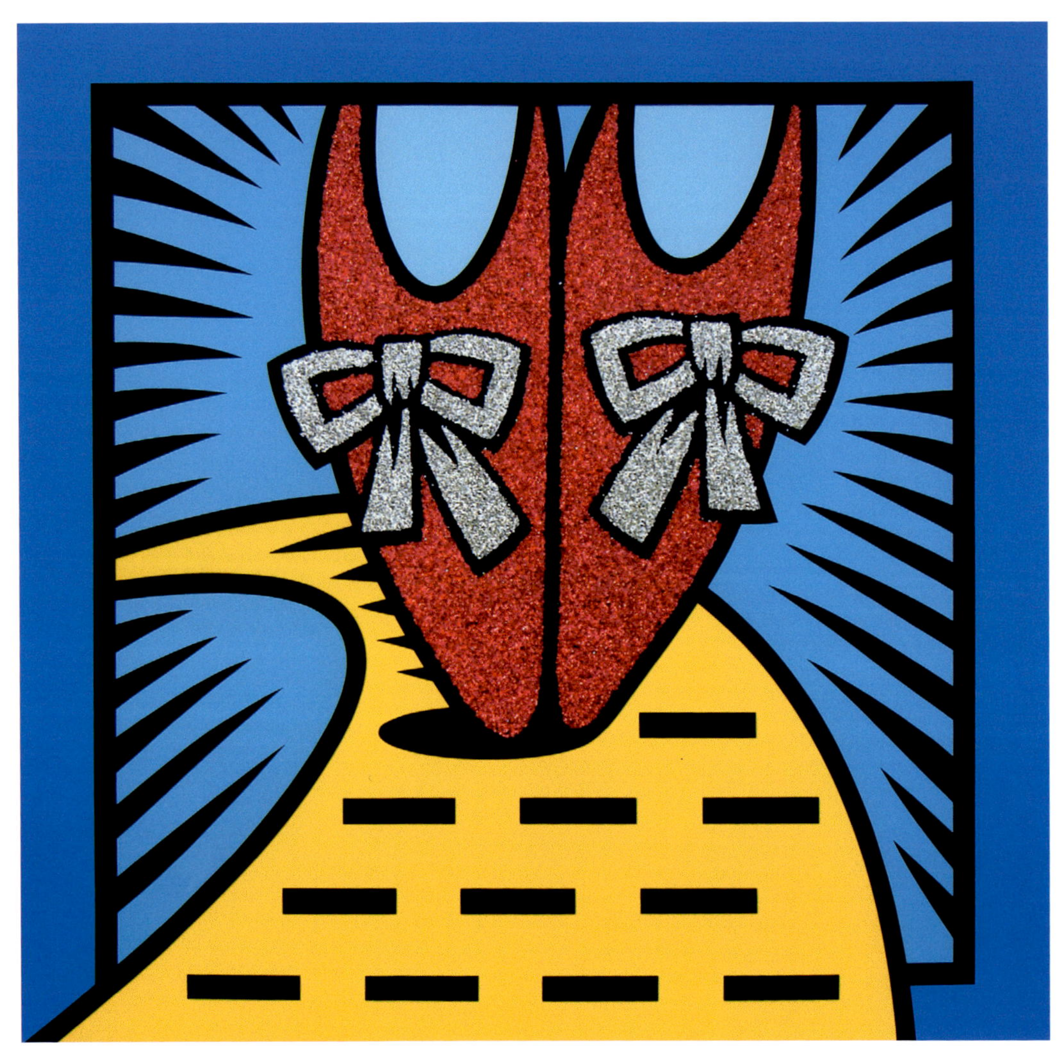

No Place Like Home
2003
Silkscreen ink on gesso board
with hand glitter
22 x 22 inches
(55.88 x 55.88 cm)

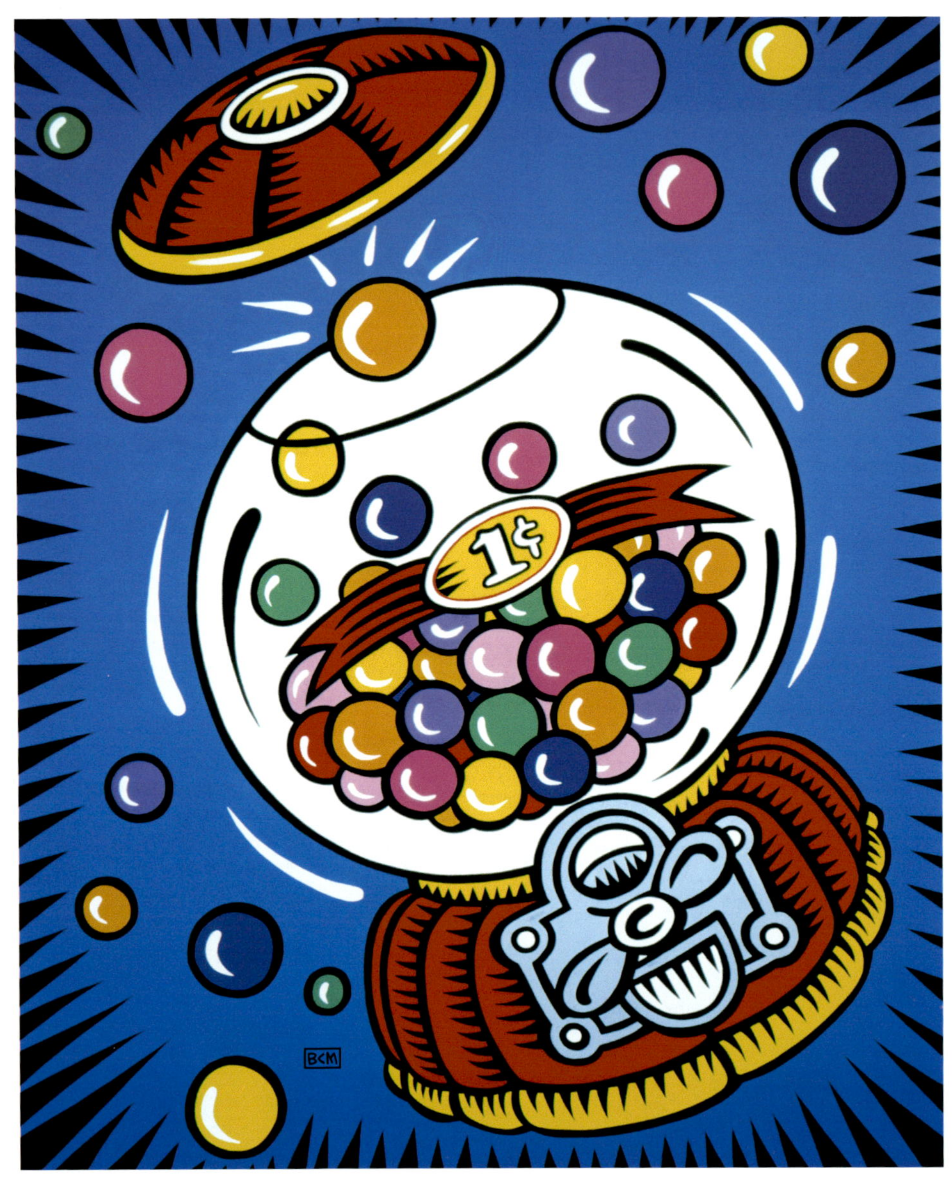

Penny–A–Pop
2003
Acrylic paint on canvas
60 x 48 inches
(152.4 x 121.92 cm)

"Thanks for using your art in helping children
to learn and grow—to love and to be real."

FRED ROGERS
Mr. Roger's Neighborhood

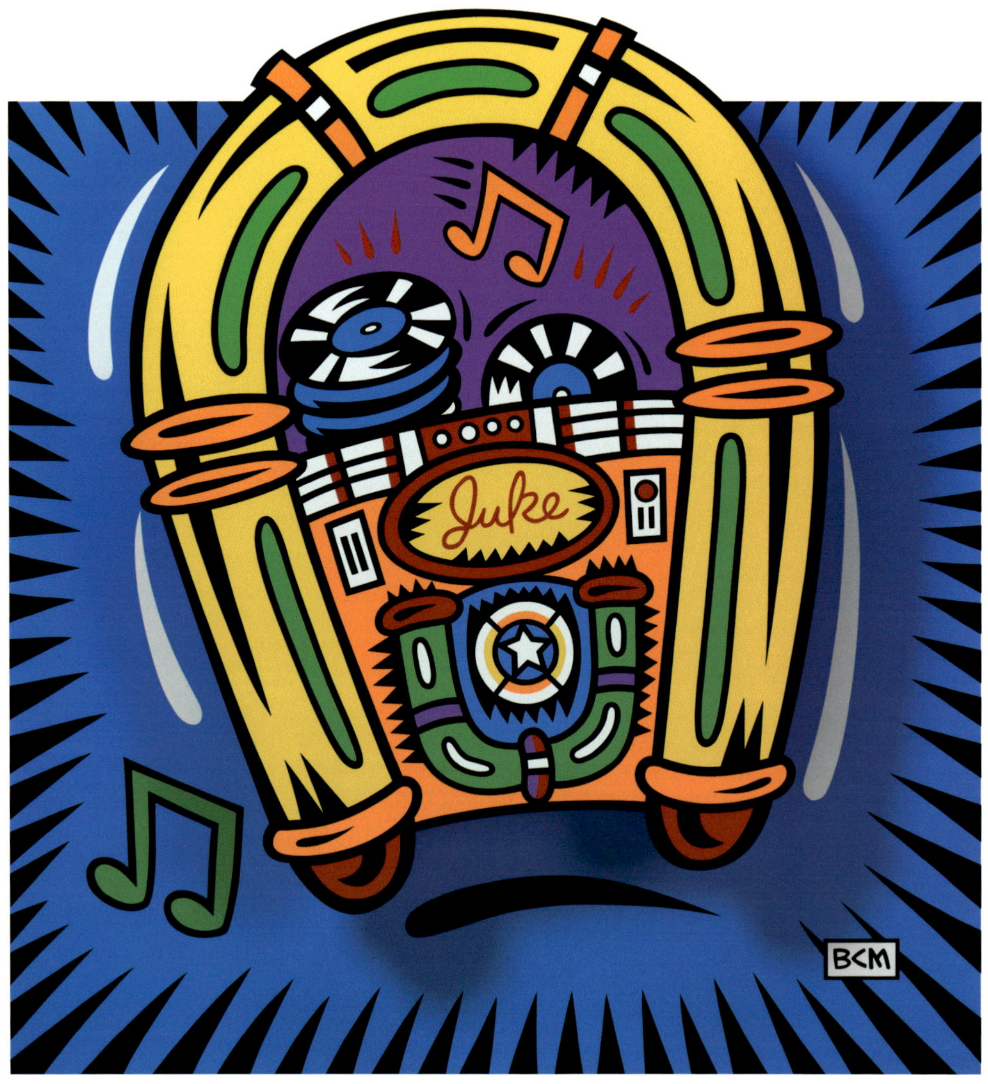
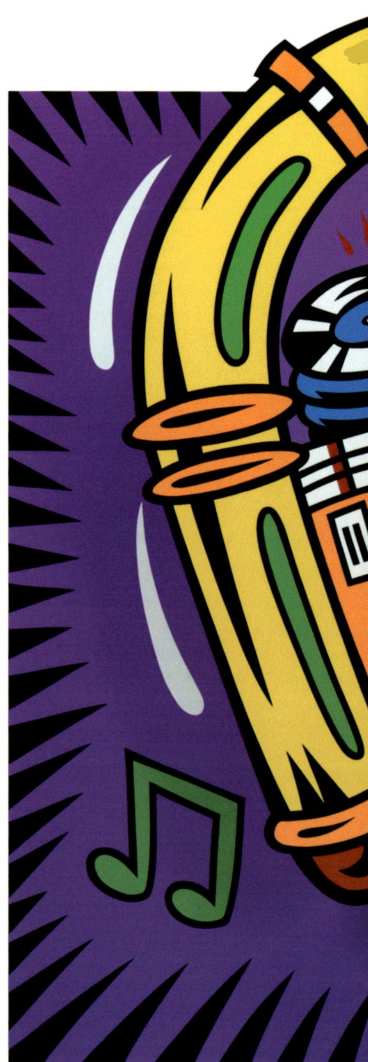

Jumpin' Juke
2004
Silkscreen ink on gesso board
with dimensional pop-out front panel
Edition of 17
24 x 24 x 4 inches
(60.96 x 60.96 x 10.16 cm)

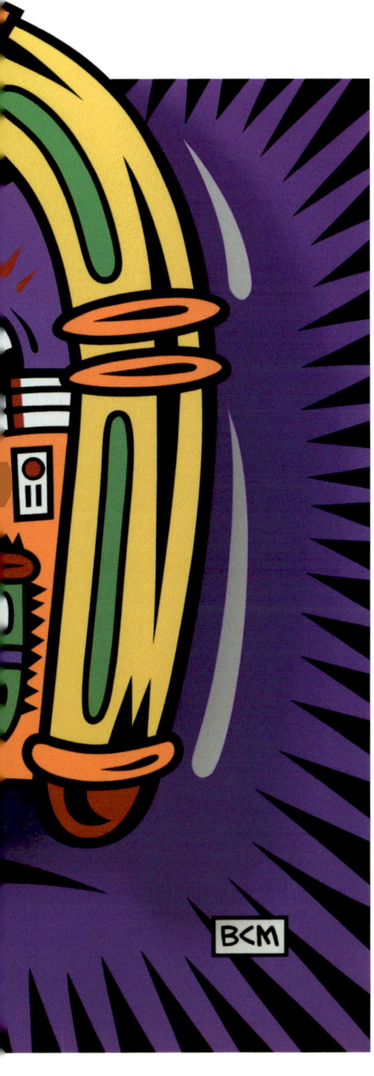
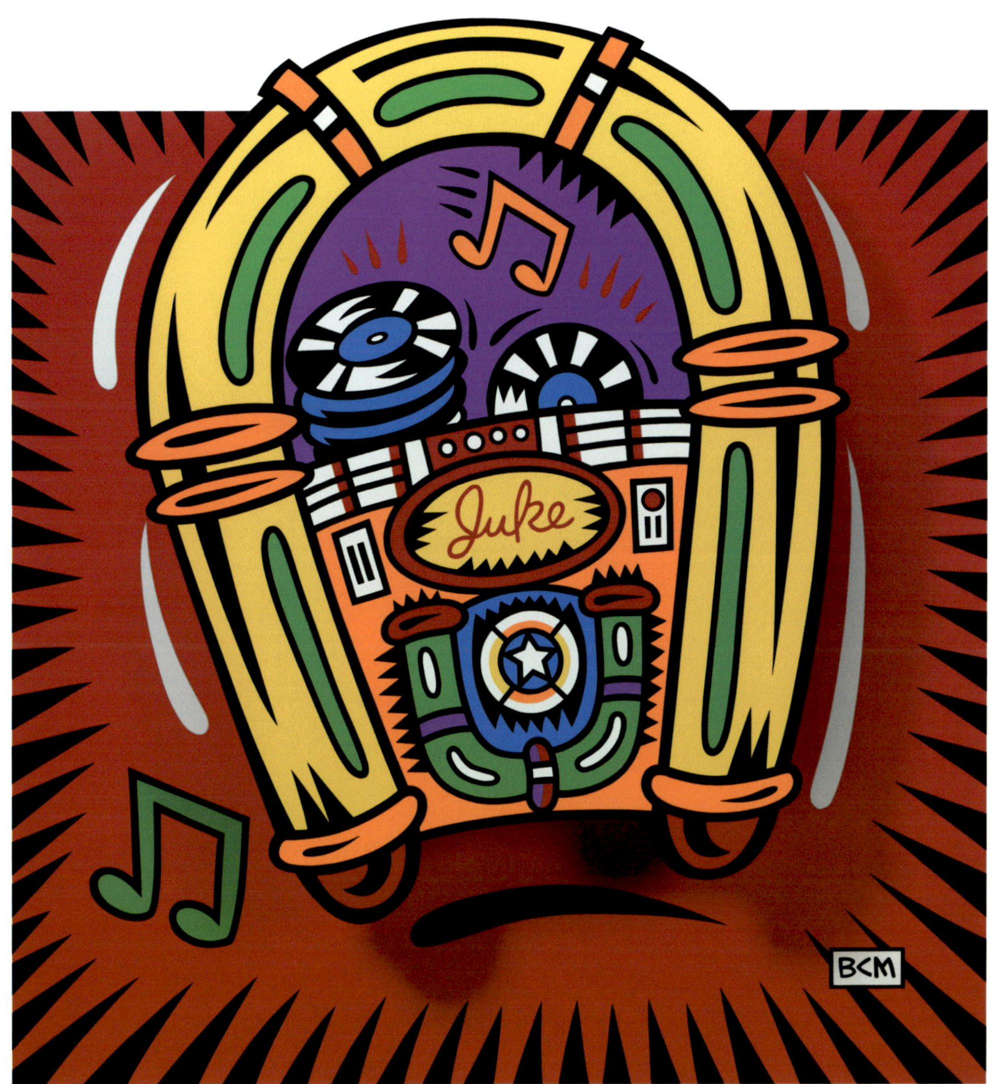
Juke
BCM

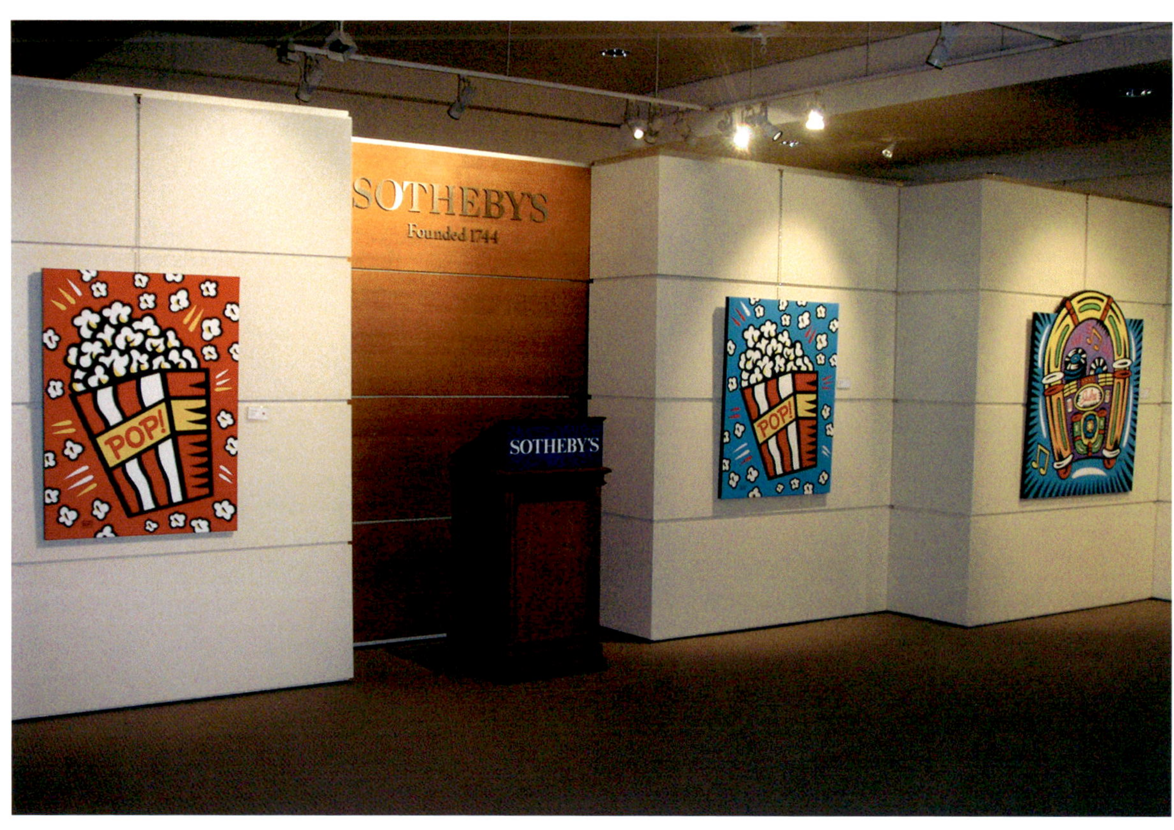

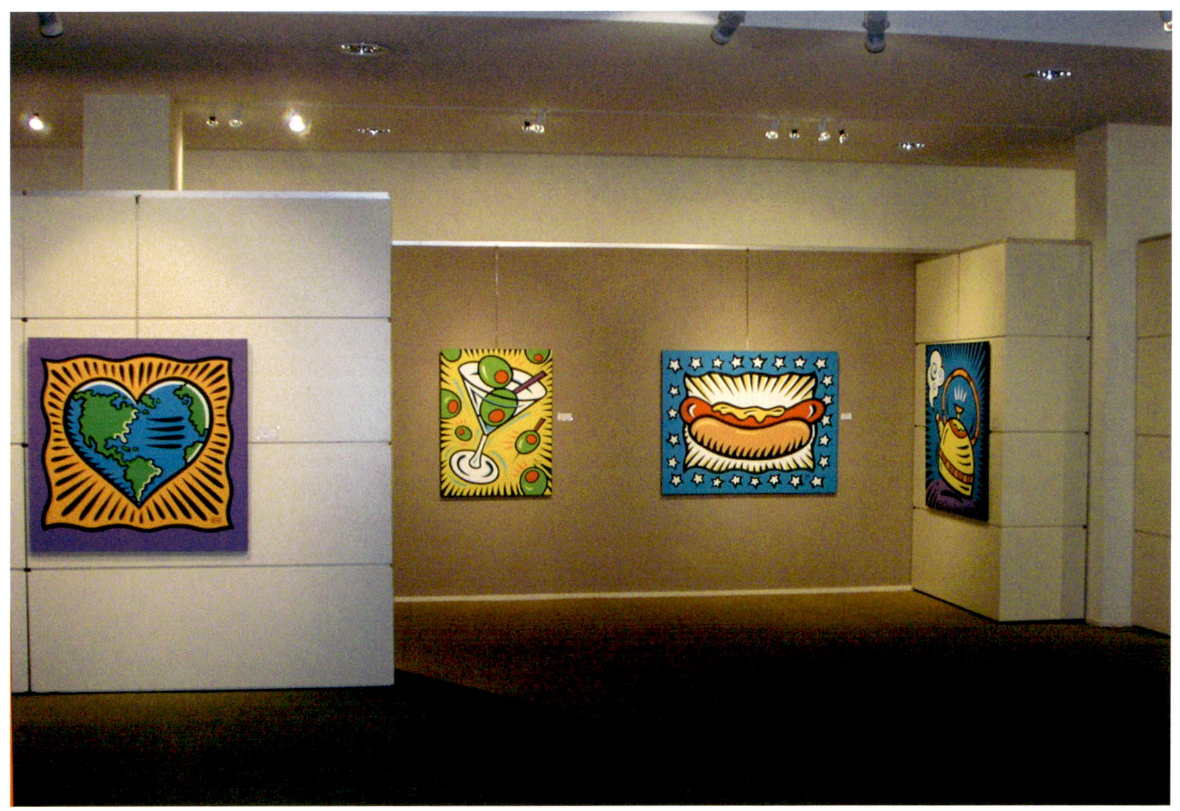

Sotheby's
2003
Amsterdam, The Netherlands

Pop! Pop! Pop!
2003
Acrylic paint on canvas
20 x 16 x 3 inches each
(50.8 x 40.64 x 7.62 cm each)

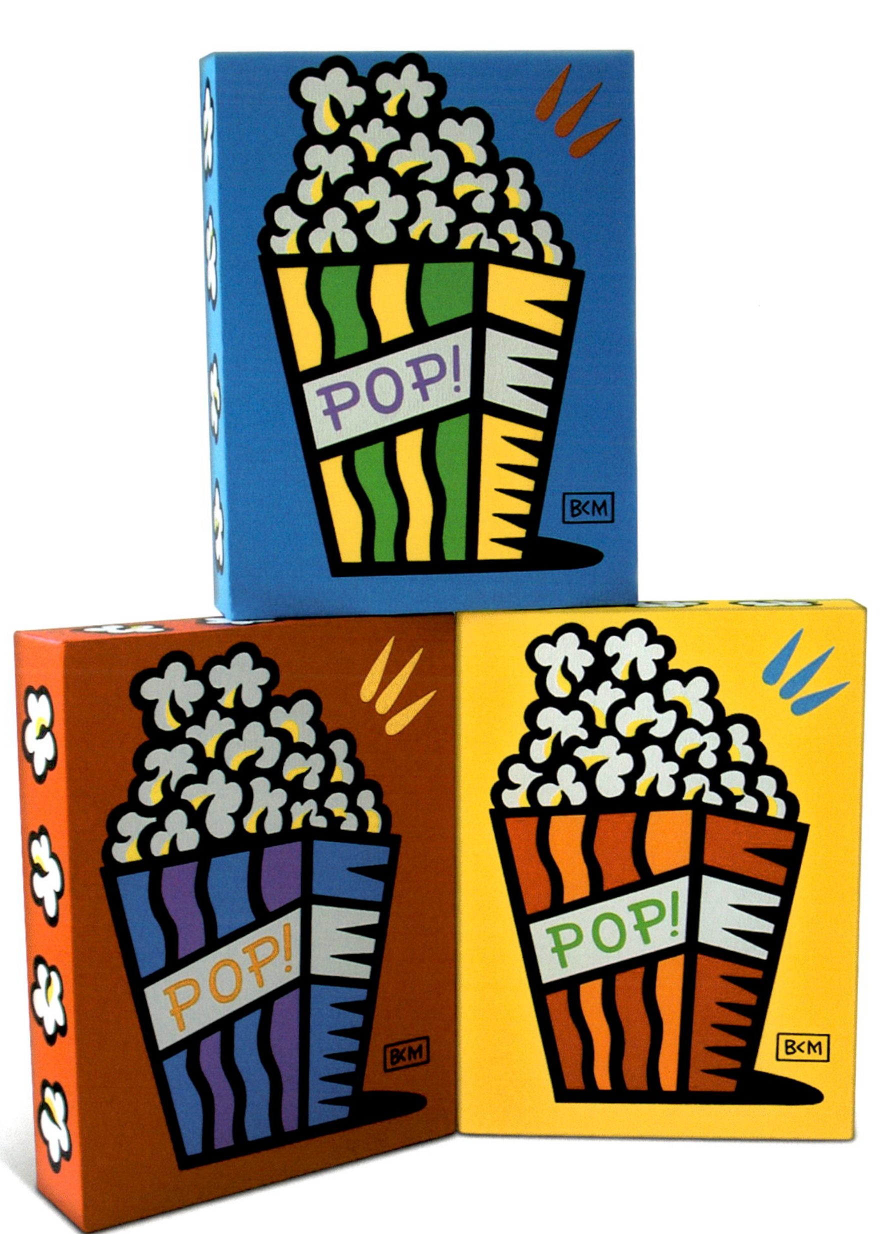
POP!
BCM
POP!
BCM
POP!
BCM

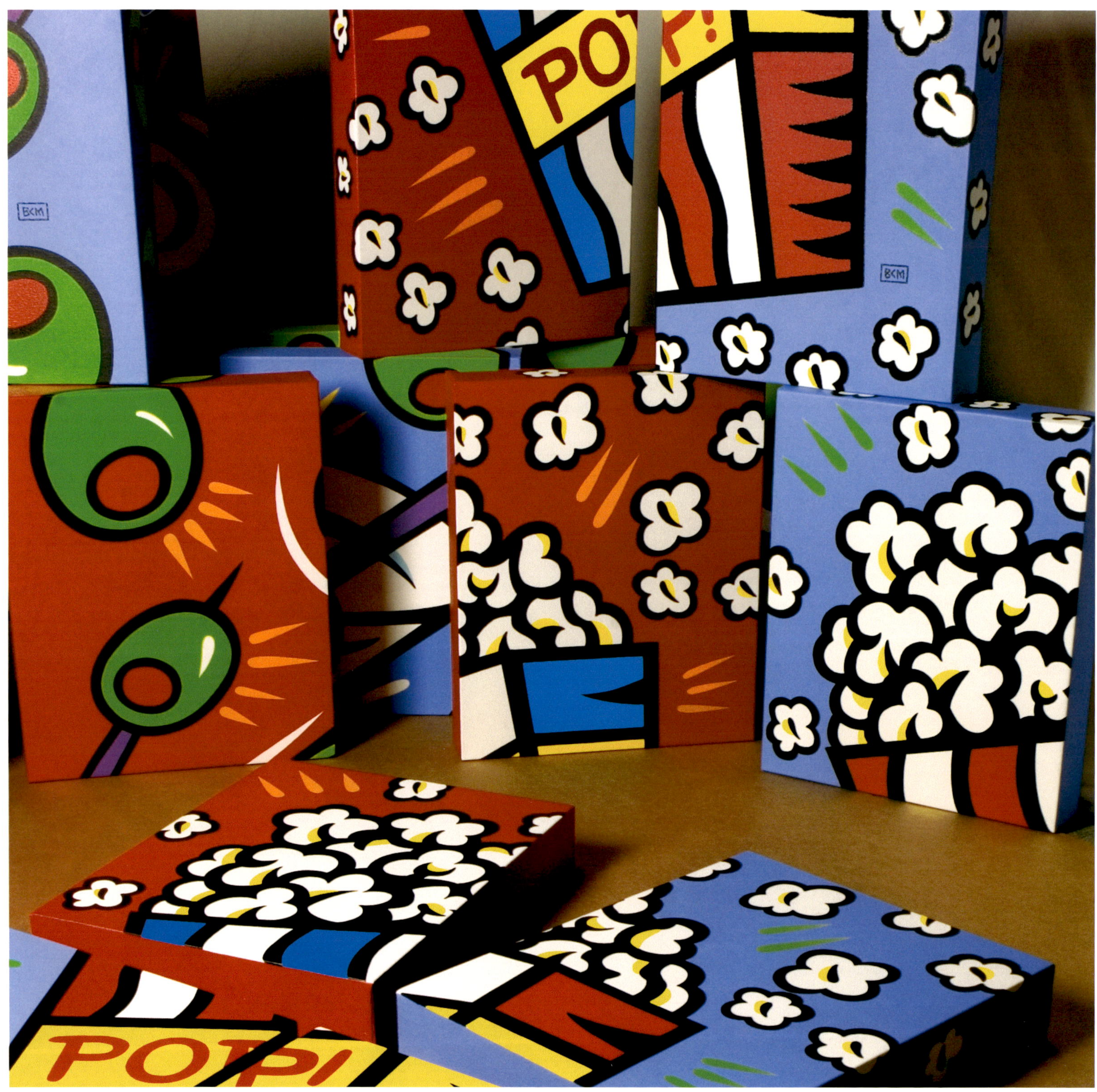

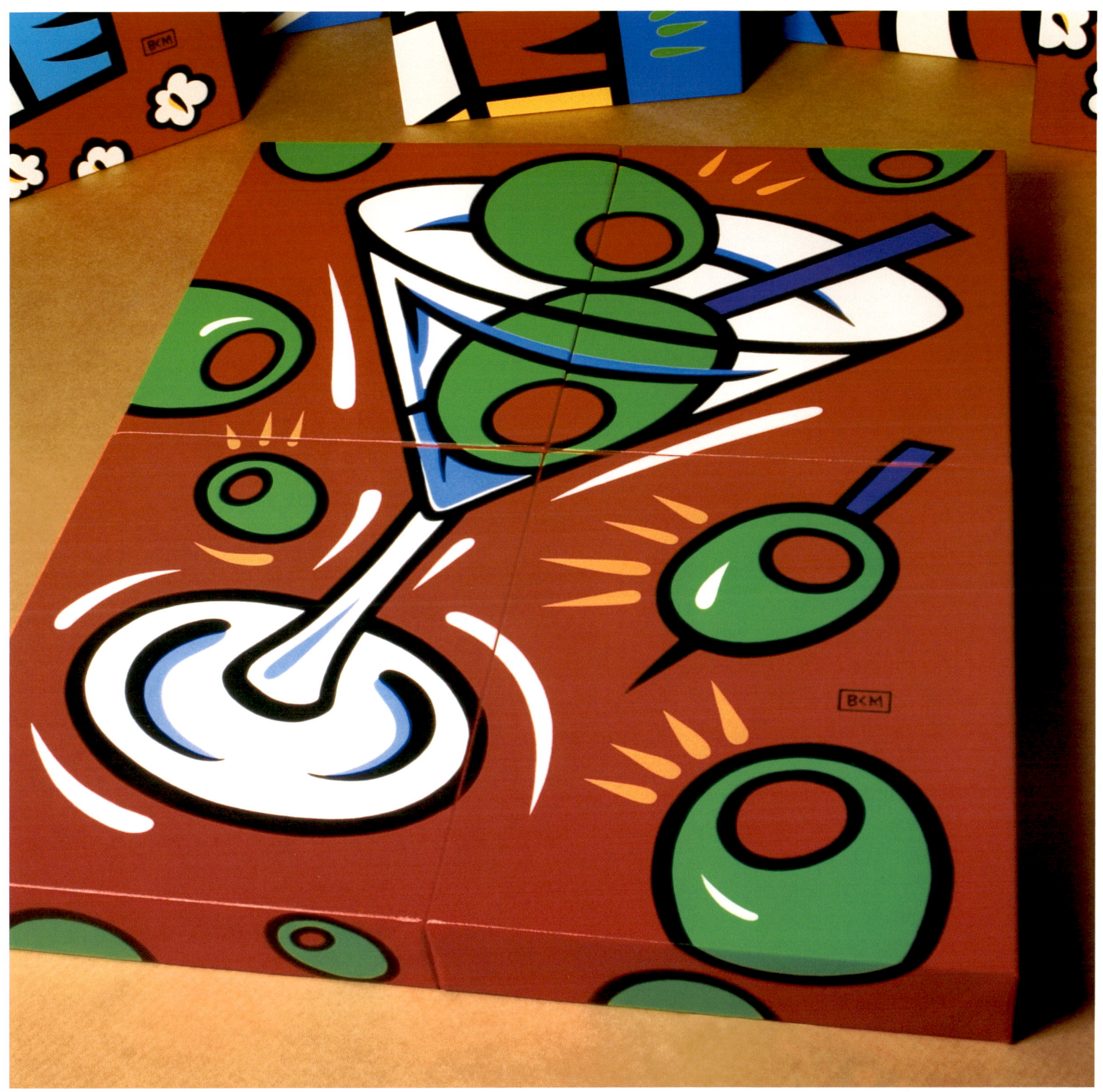

Martini Quad (previous page)
2007
Acrylic paint on canvas
40 x 32 x 3 inches
(101.6 x 81.28 x 7.62 cm)

Pop! Quad
2007
Acrylic paint on canvas
40 x 32 x 3 inches
(101.6 x 81.28 x 7.62 cm)

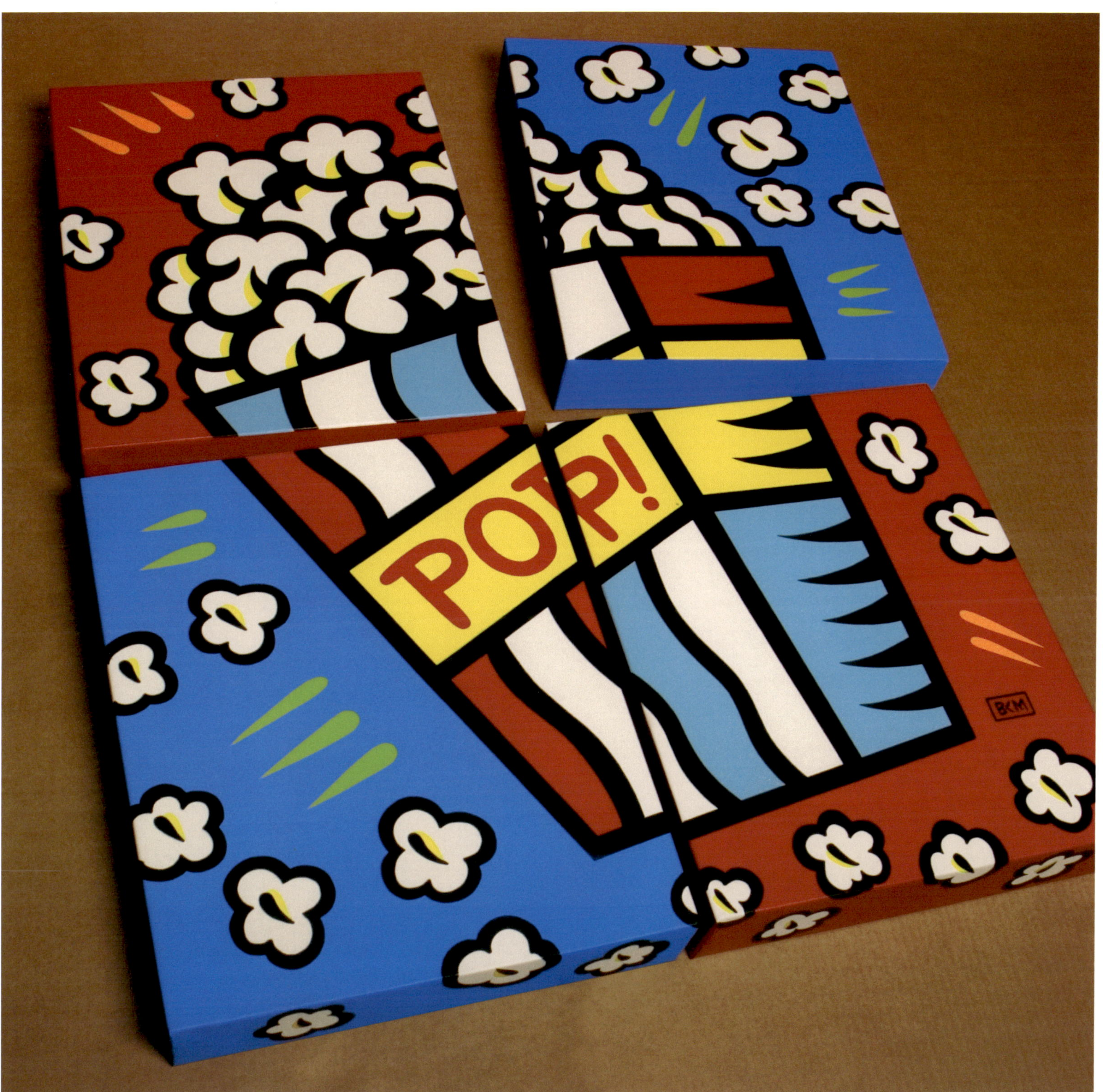

POP!
BCM

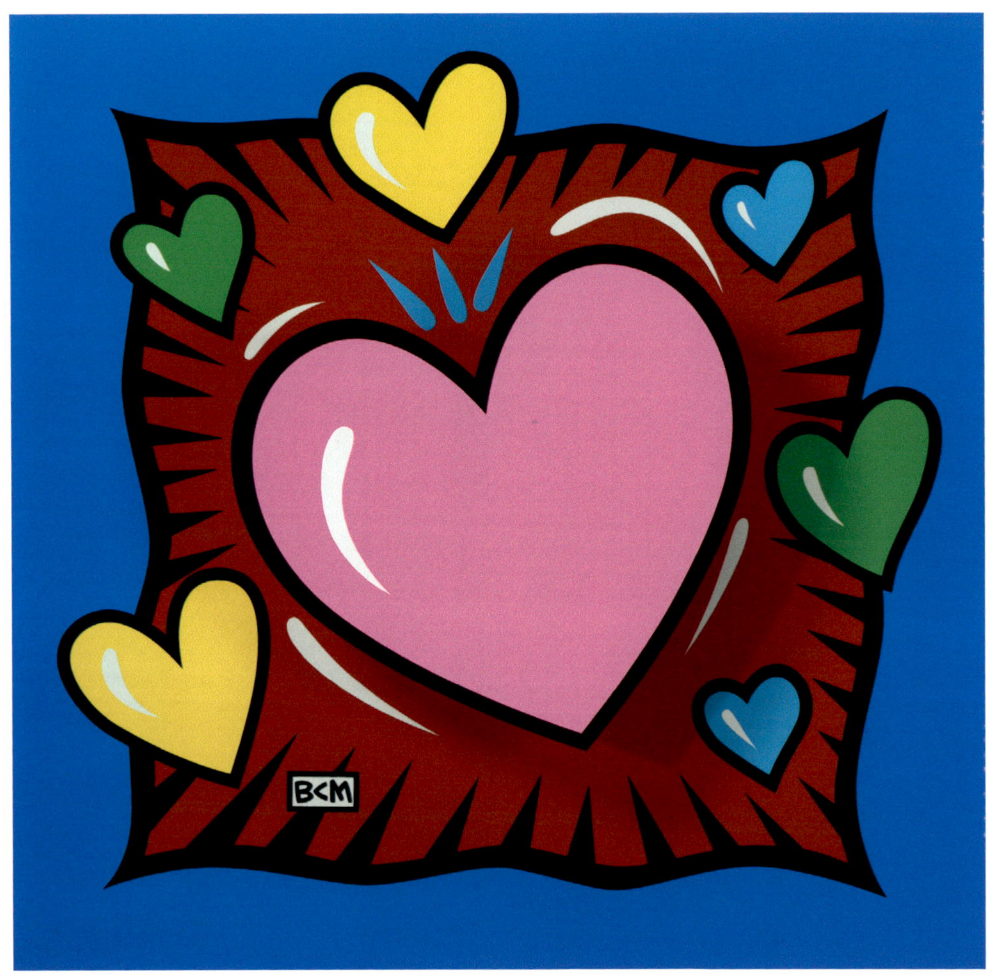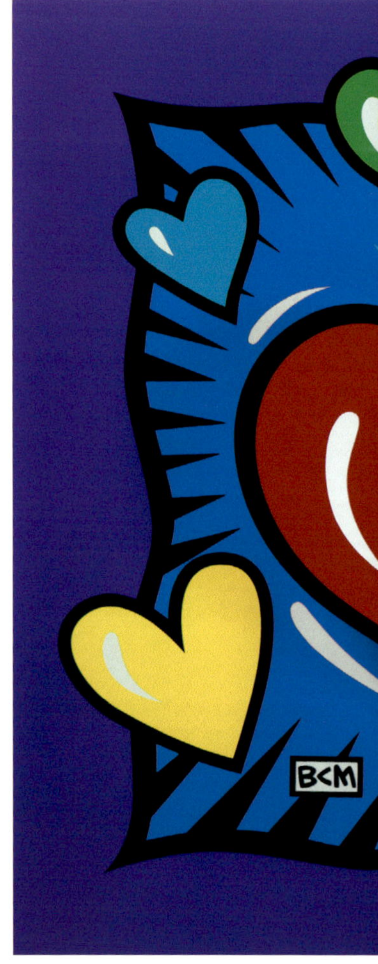

I Love You
2006
Silkscreen ink on gesso board
with dimensional pop-out front panel
Edition of 18
24 x 24 x 4 inches
(60.96 x 60.96 x 10.16 cm)

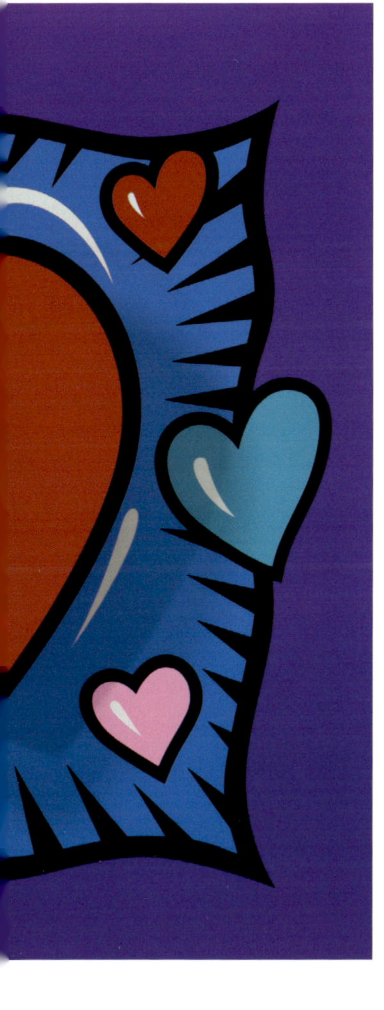
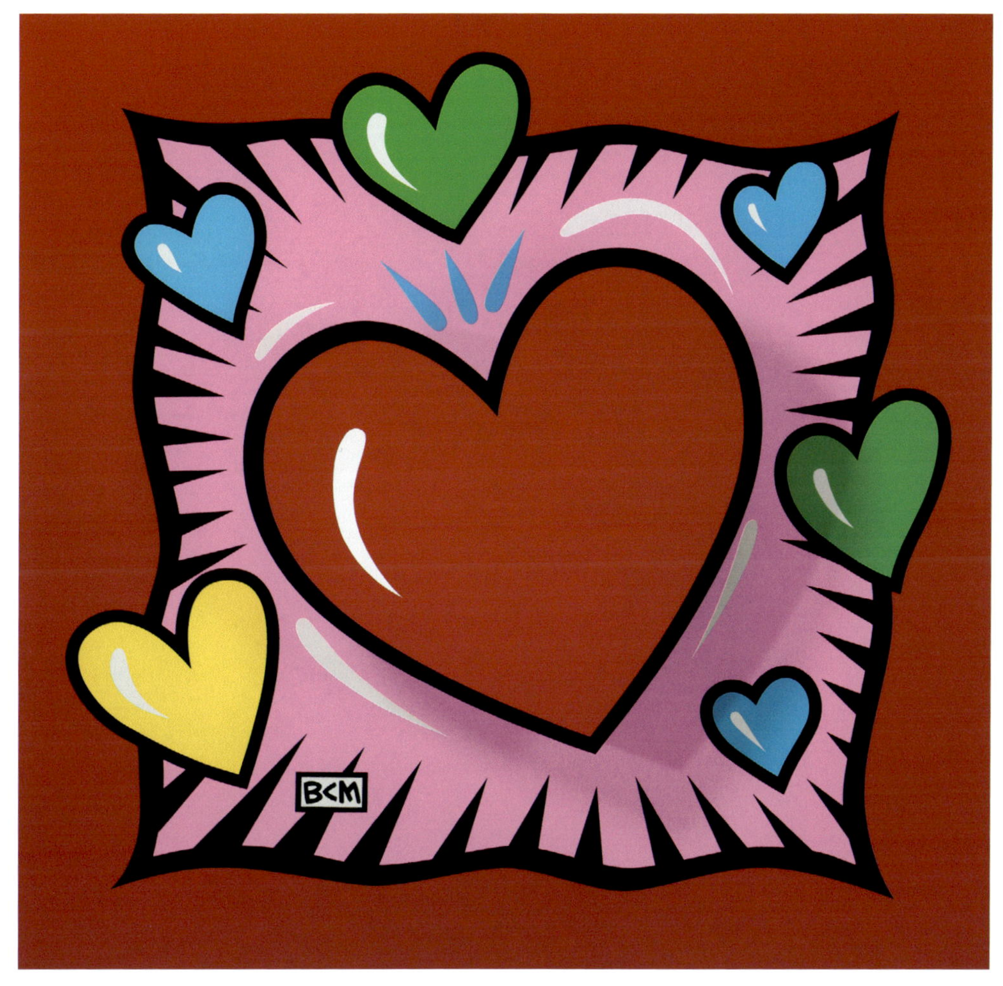

BCM

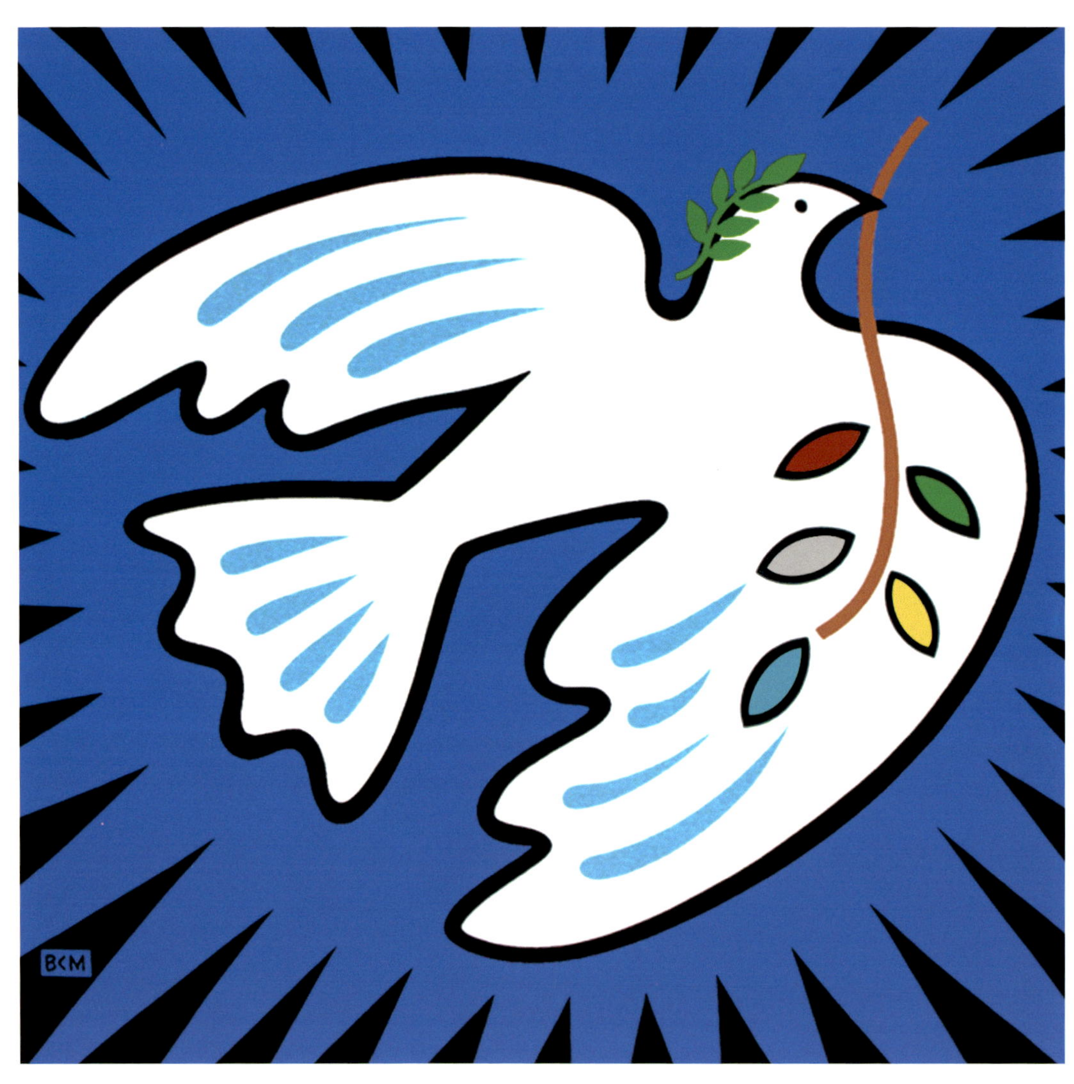

Olympic Peace Dove
2004
Acrylic paint on canvas
36 x 36 inches
(91.44 x 91.44 cm)

"It was a real pleasure and an honour for the Olympic Museum to present an exhibition in 2004 devoted entirely to Burton Morris.

This exhibition, entitled "The Spirit of the Game", displayed about 30 original works, inspired by three fundamental themes of Olympism: the Games of Antiquity, the symbols and the athletes.

Burton Morris was able, on this occasion, to interpret the Olympic spirit in its own artistic language with much impact and originality. It gave us a popular view, full of youthfulness and enthusiasm, which appealed to the Museum's local and international visitors.

Thanks once again to Burton Morris for this breath of fresh air and modernity which he gave to Olympism."

FRANCIS GABET
Director
International Olympic Museum

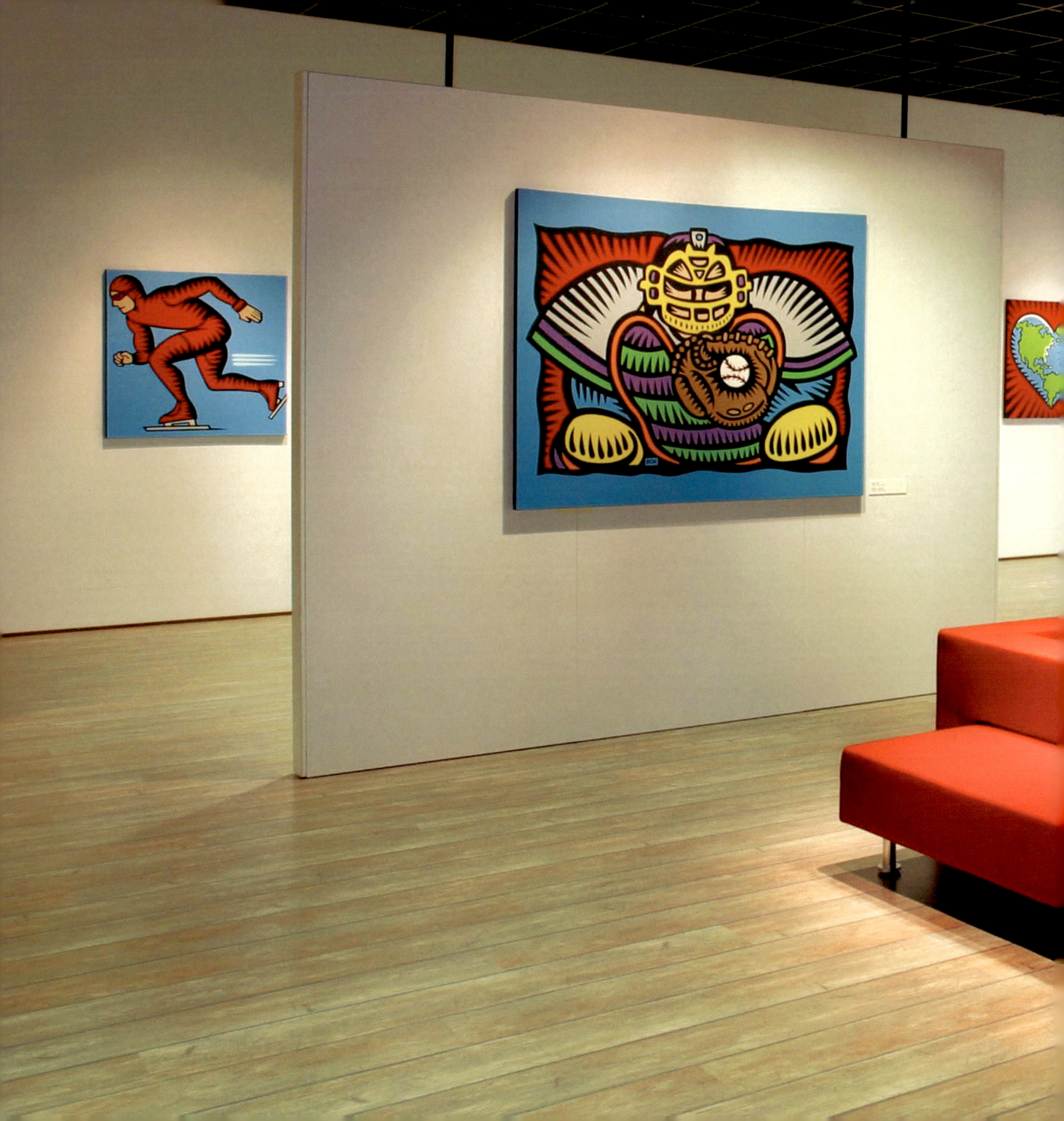

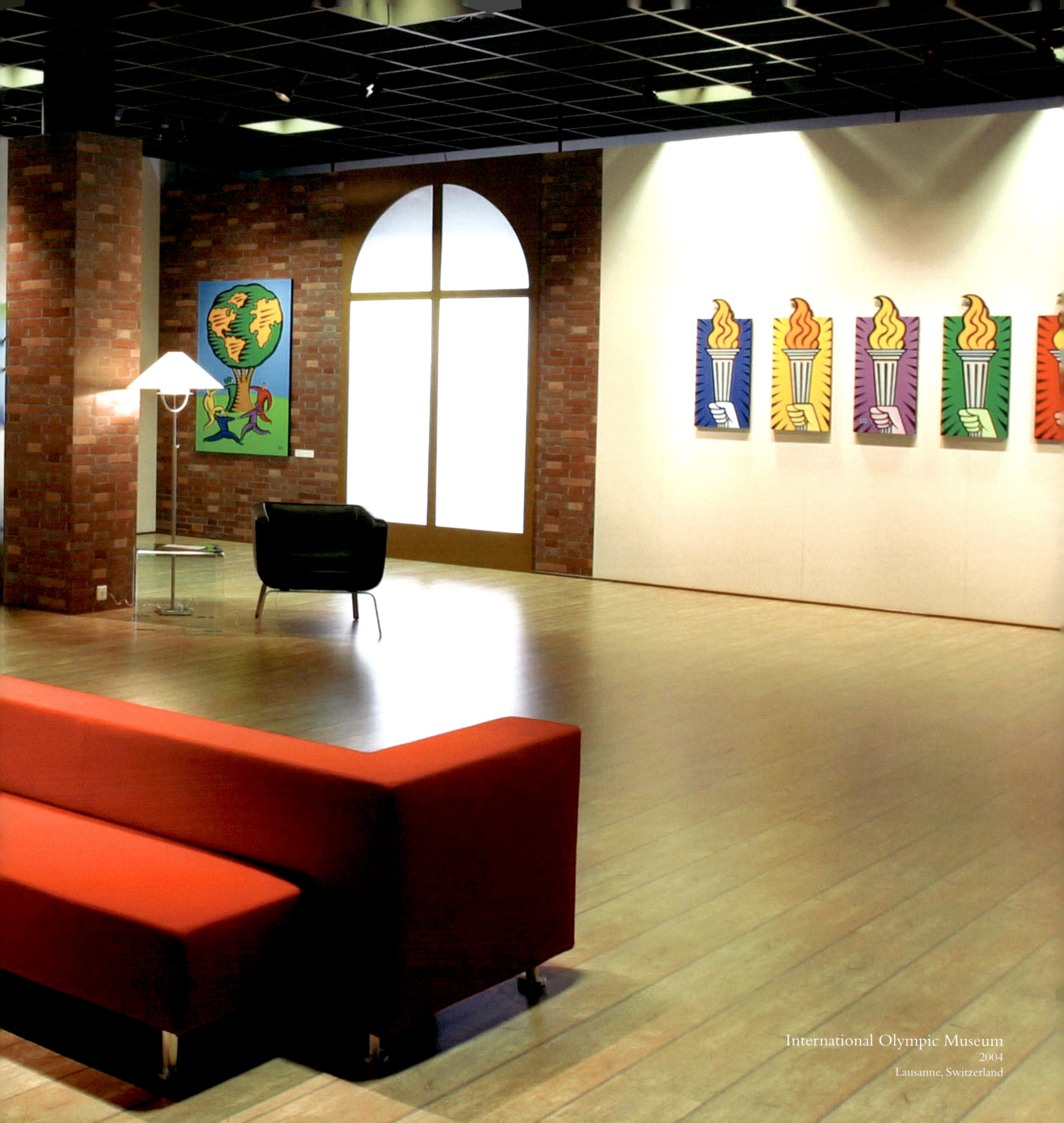

International Olympic Museum
2004
Lausanne, Switzerland

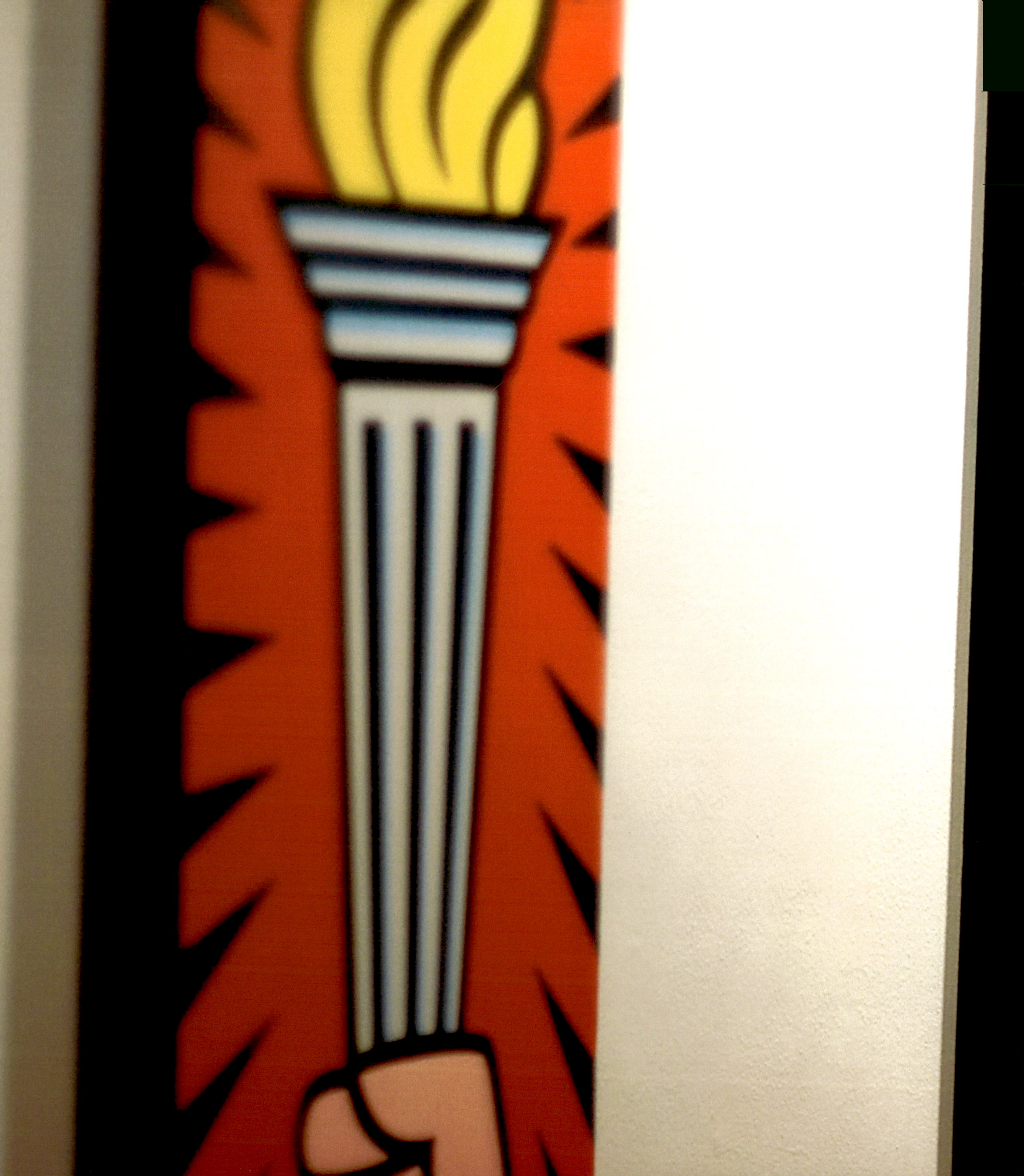

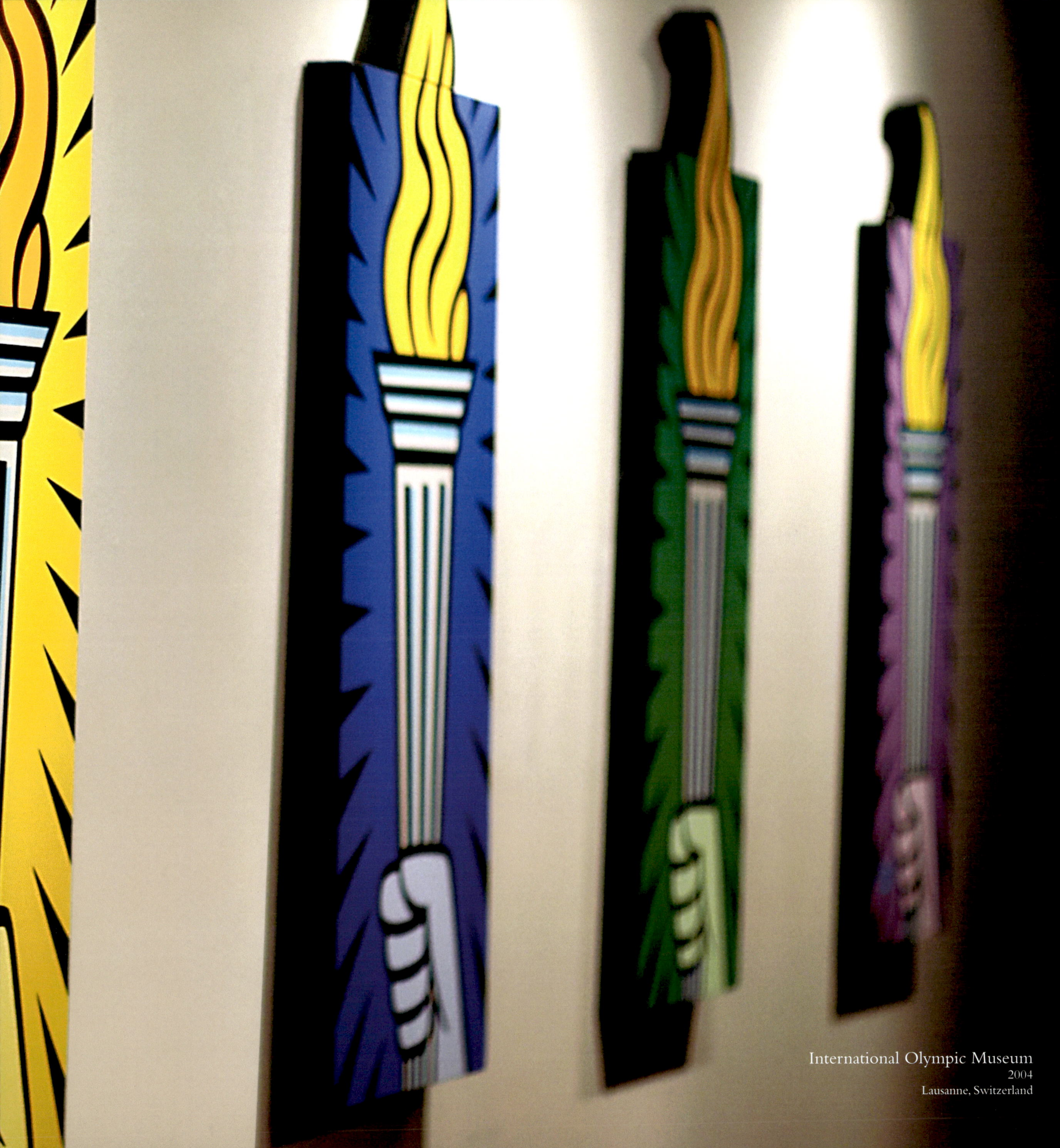

International Olympic Museum
2004
Lausanne, Switzerland

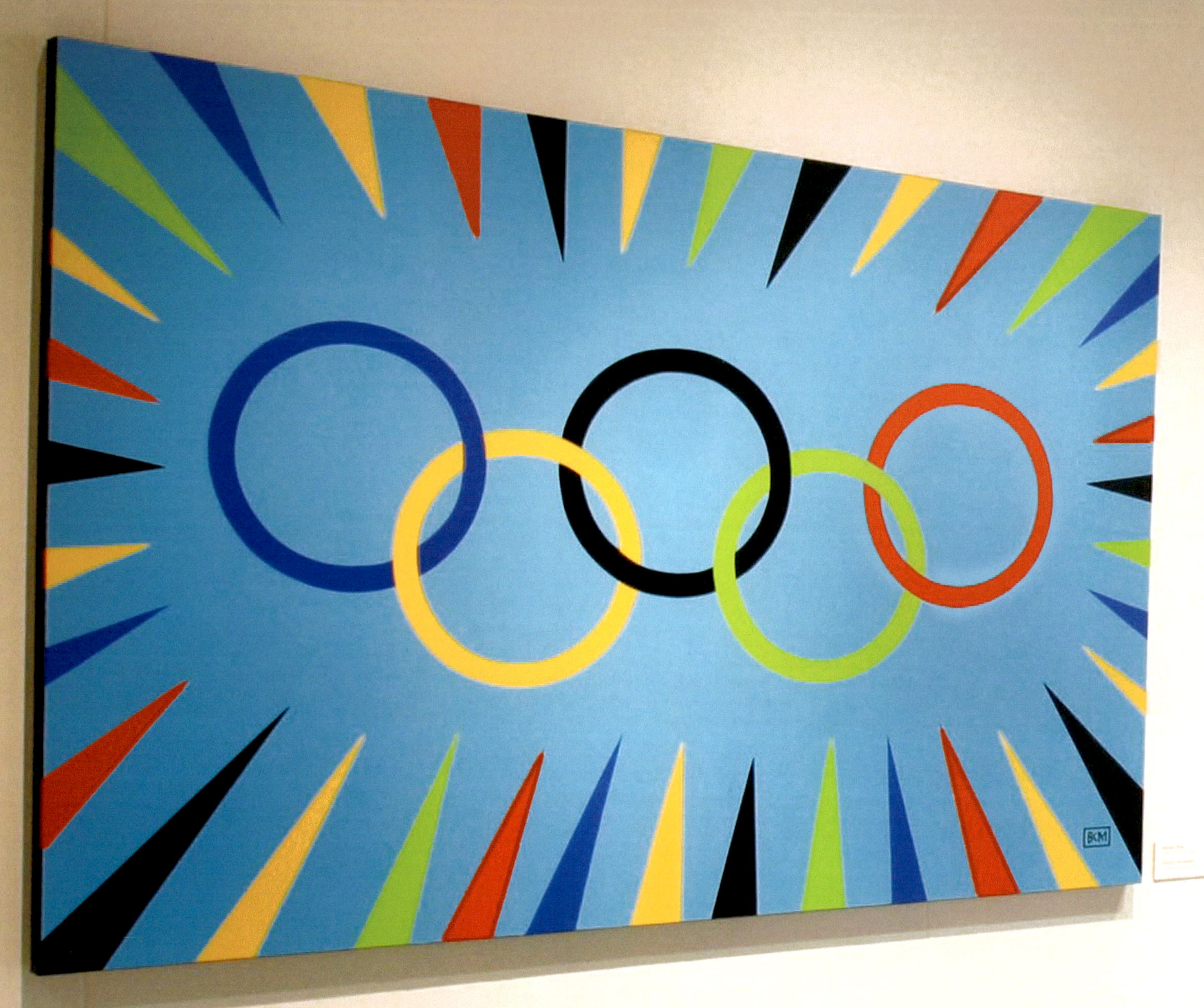

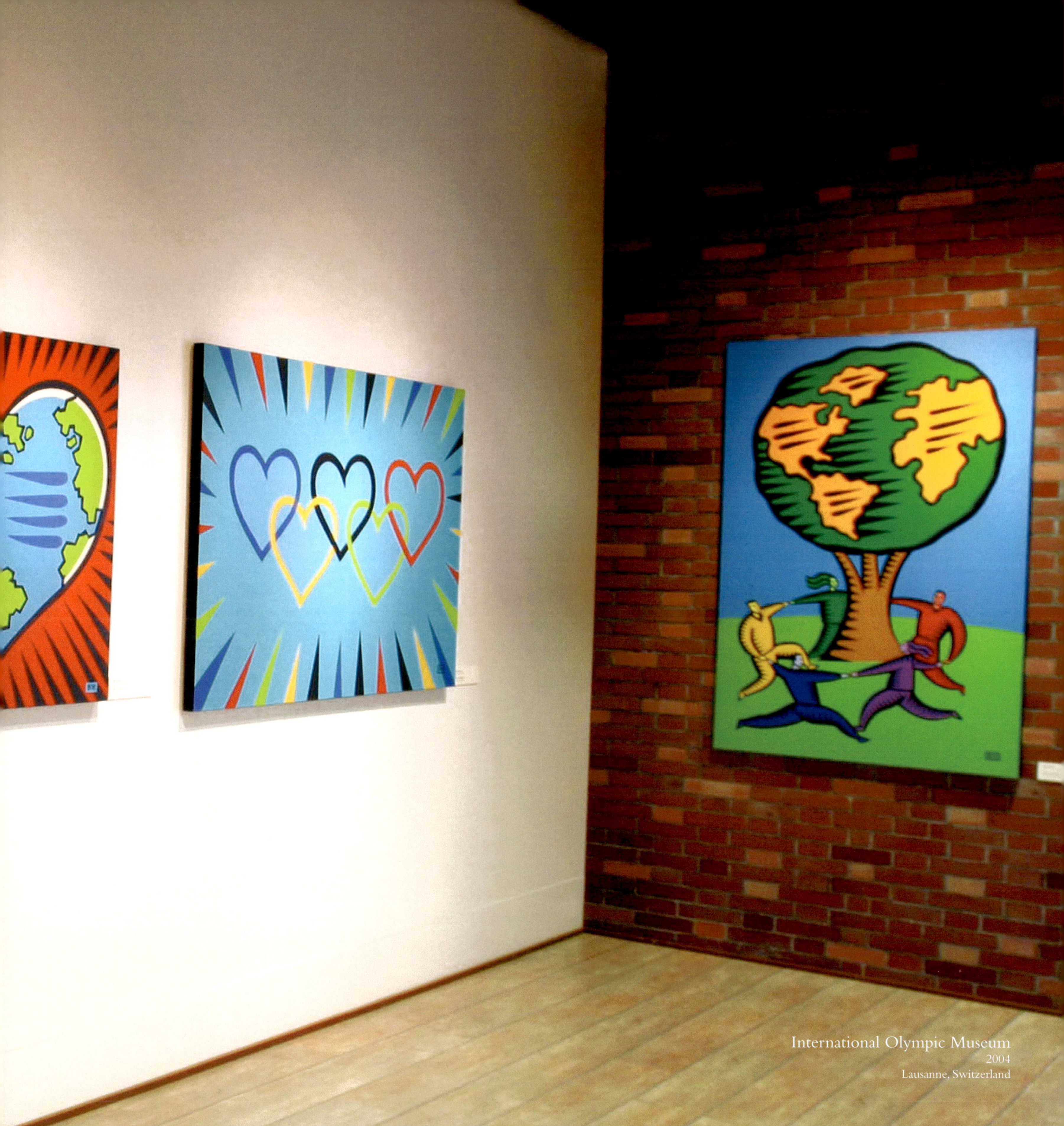

International Olympic Museum
2004
Lausanne, Switzerland

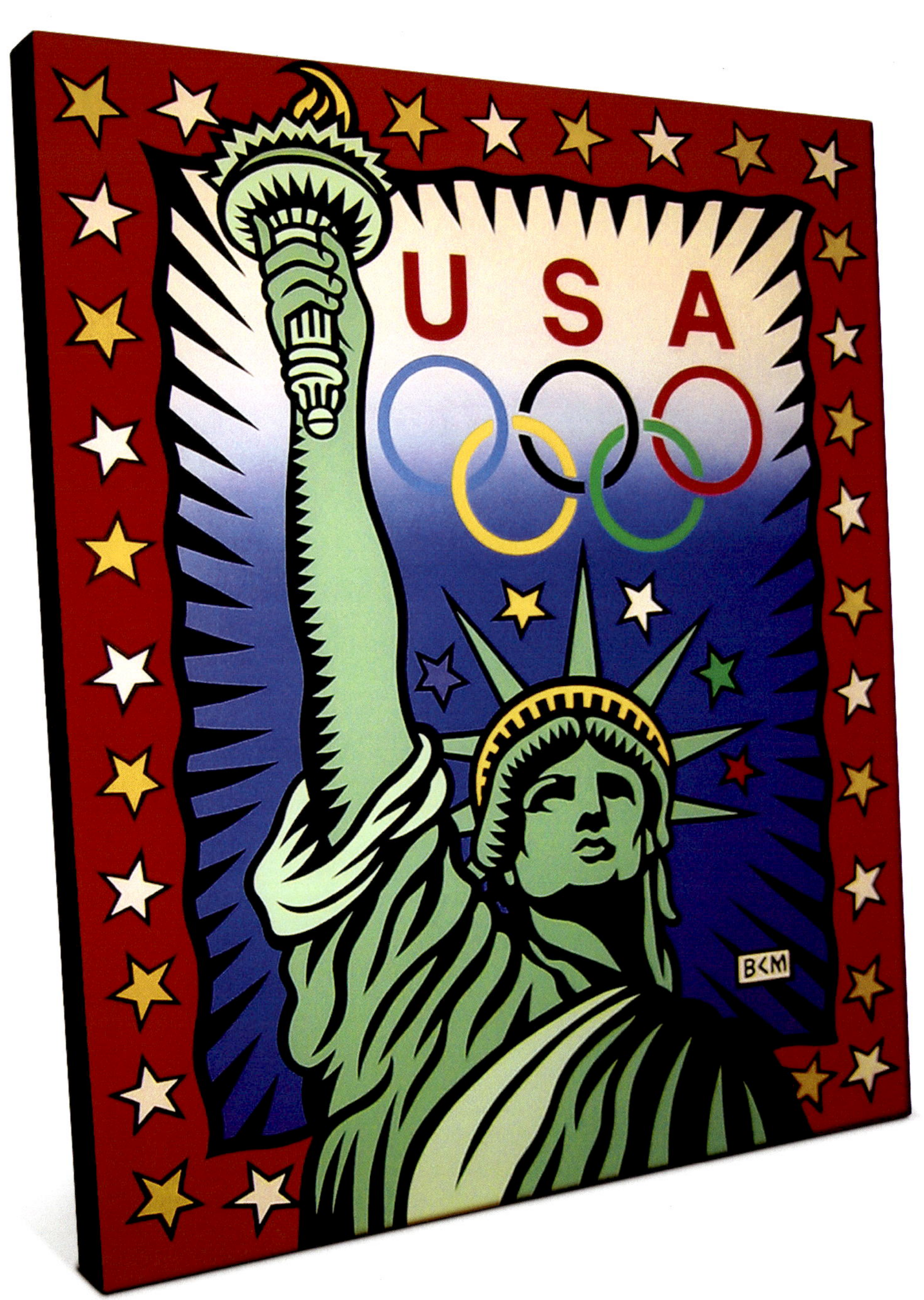

USA
BCM

US Olympic Team-Athens
2004
Acrylic paint on canvas
60 x 48 inches
(152.4 x 121.92 cm)

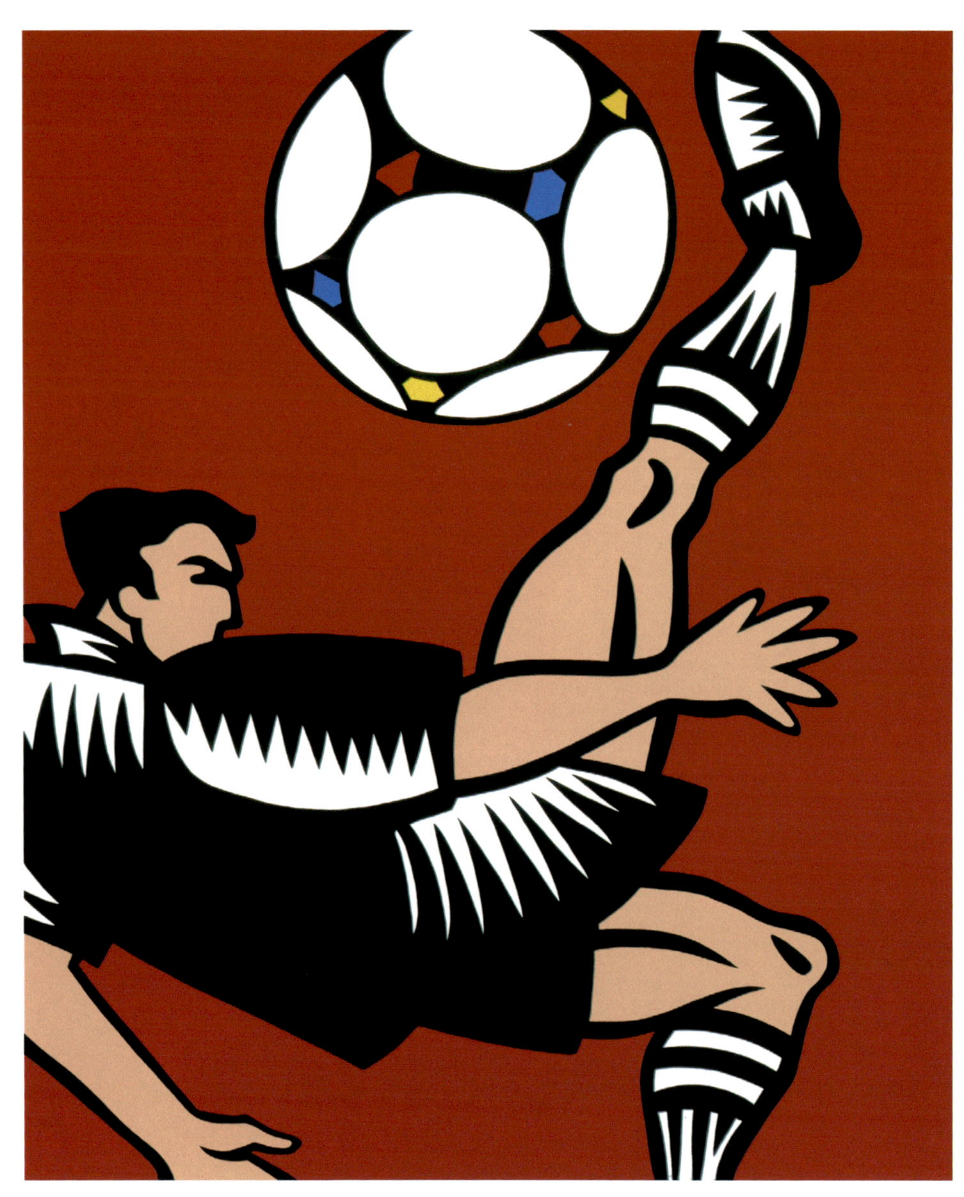

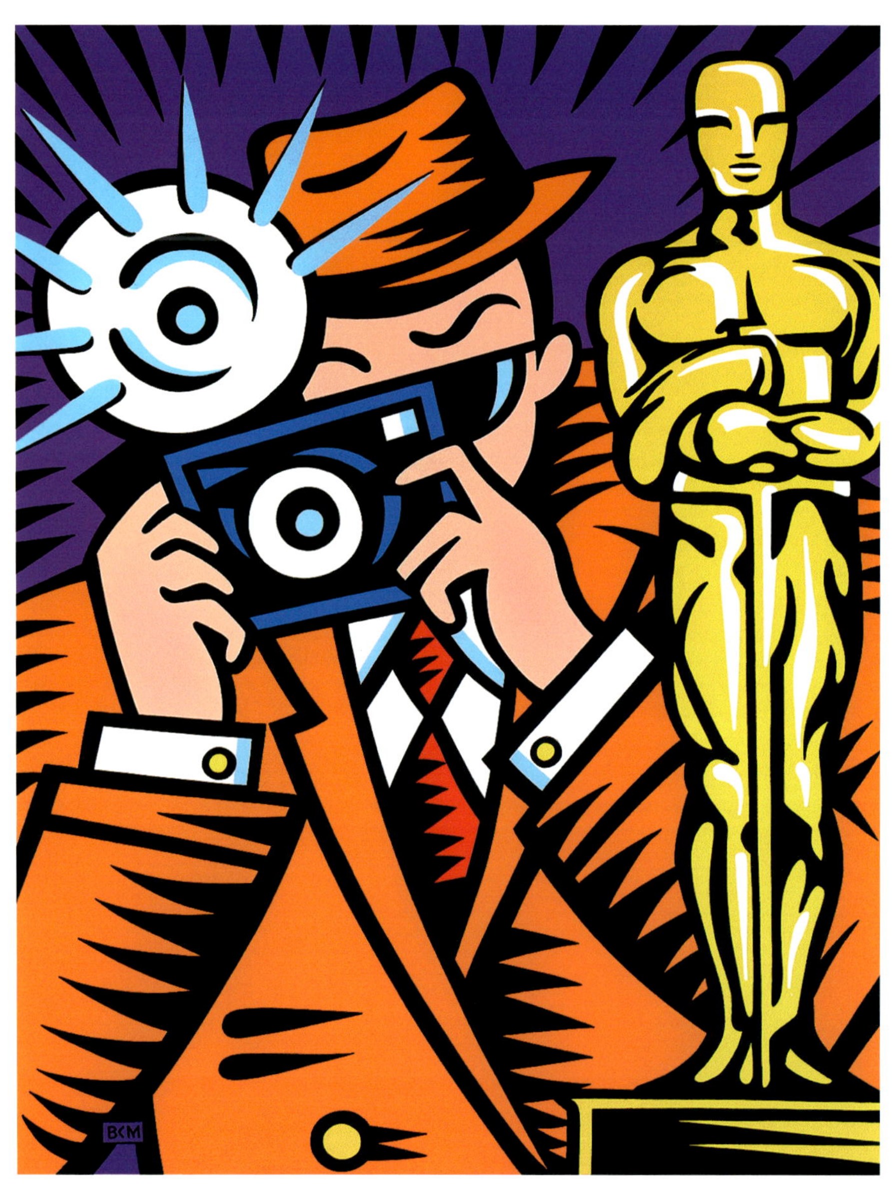

76th Annual Academy Awards
2004
Acrylic paint on canvas
48 x 36 inches
(121.92 x 91.44 cm)

"We asked Burton to come up with an image to
re-energize the Oscars and to bring back some of the
glitz, glamour, and flash of Hollywood. His artwork is
youthful and fun, and it captures the excitement
that surrounds the Academy Awards."

BRUCE DAVIS
Executive Director
Academy of Motion Picture Arts and Sciences

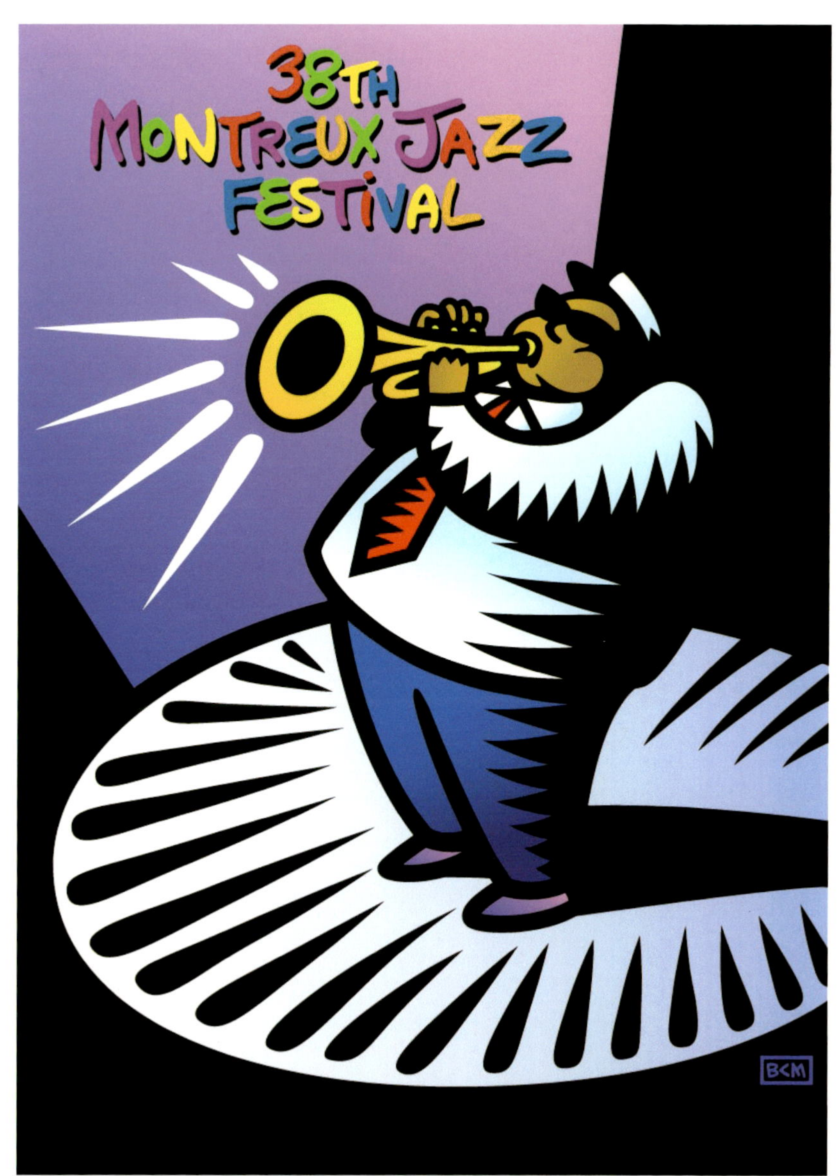

38TH
MONTREUX JAZZ
FESTIVAL
BCM

On Top of the World
2007
Acrylic paint on canvas
48 x 60 inches
(121.92 x 152.4 cm)

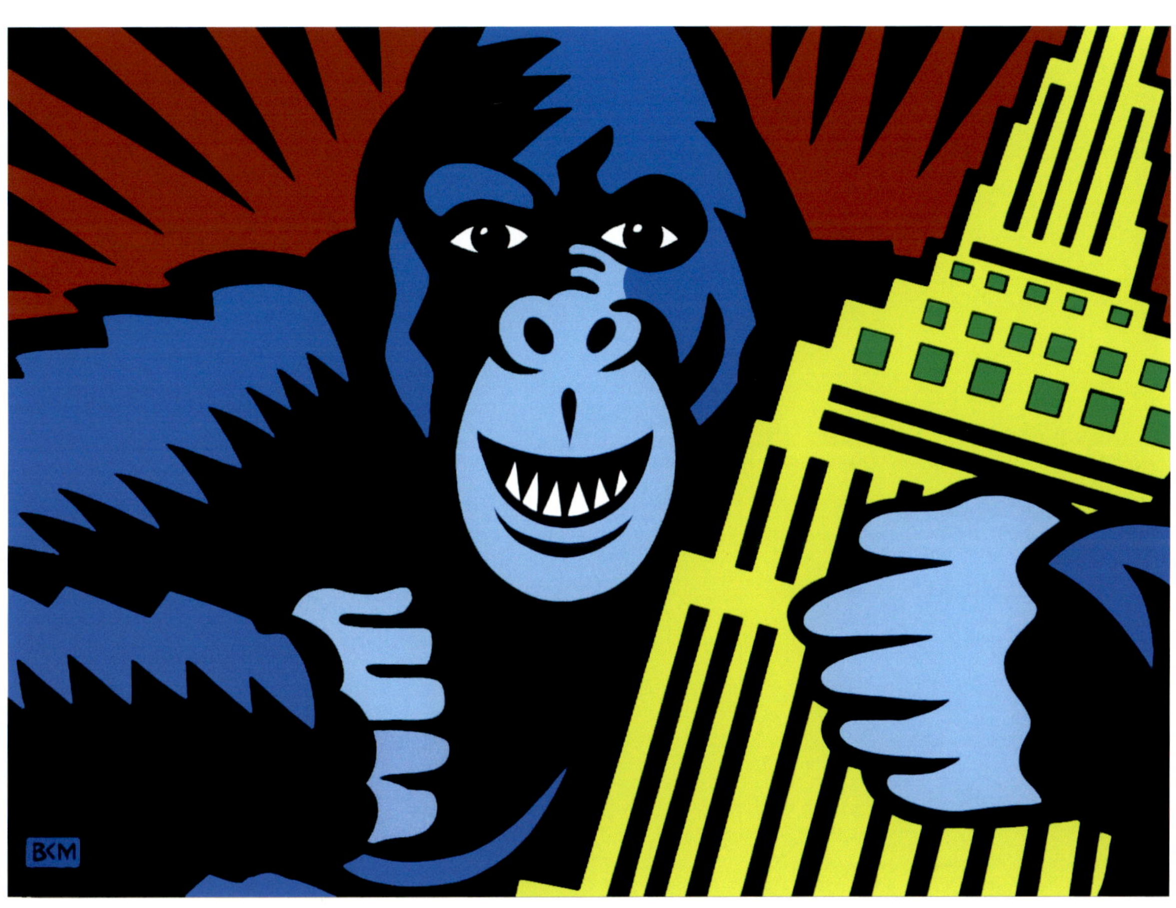

Red, White & Blue Pops!
2005
Acrylic paint on canvas
48 x 36 inches
(121.92 x 91.44 cm)

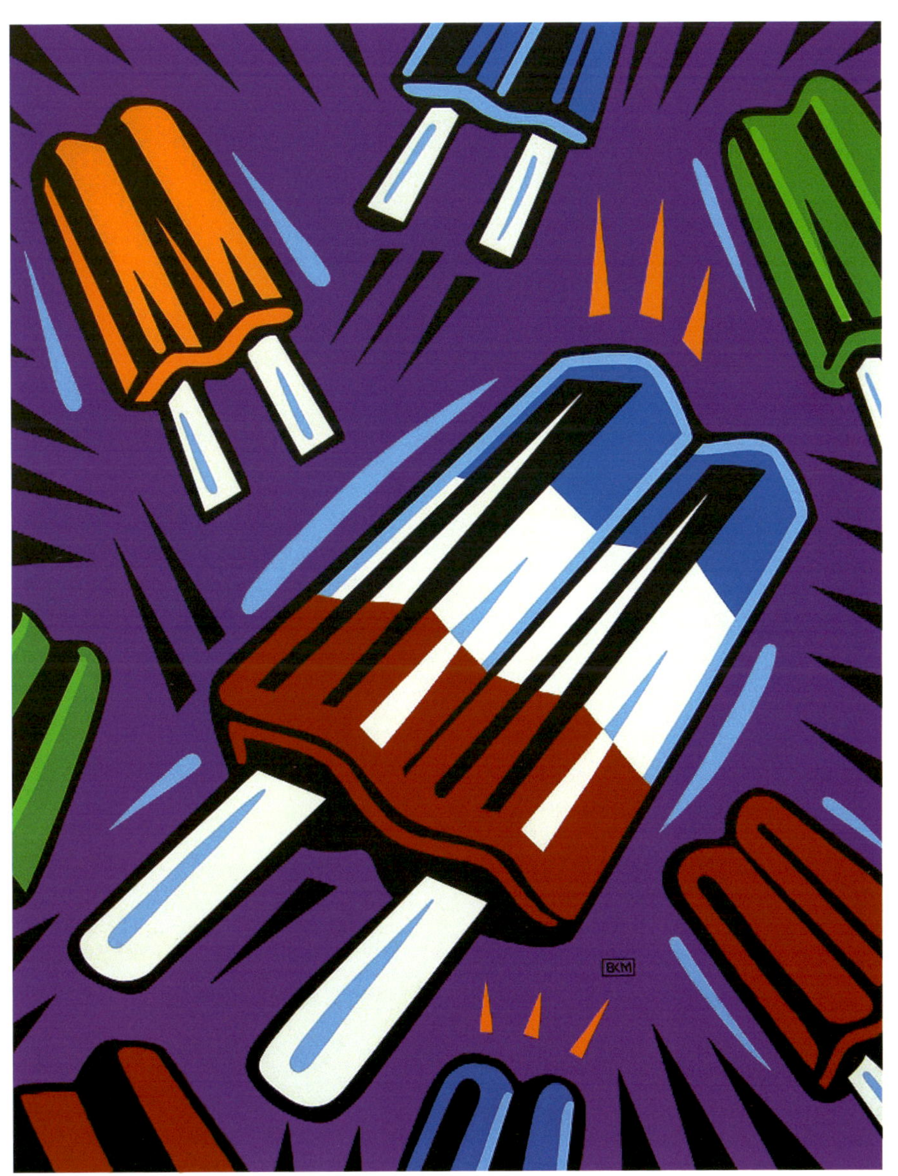

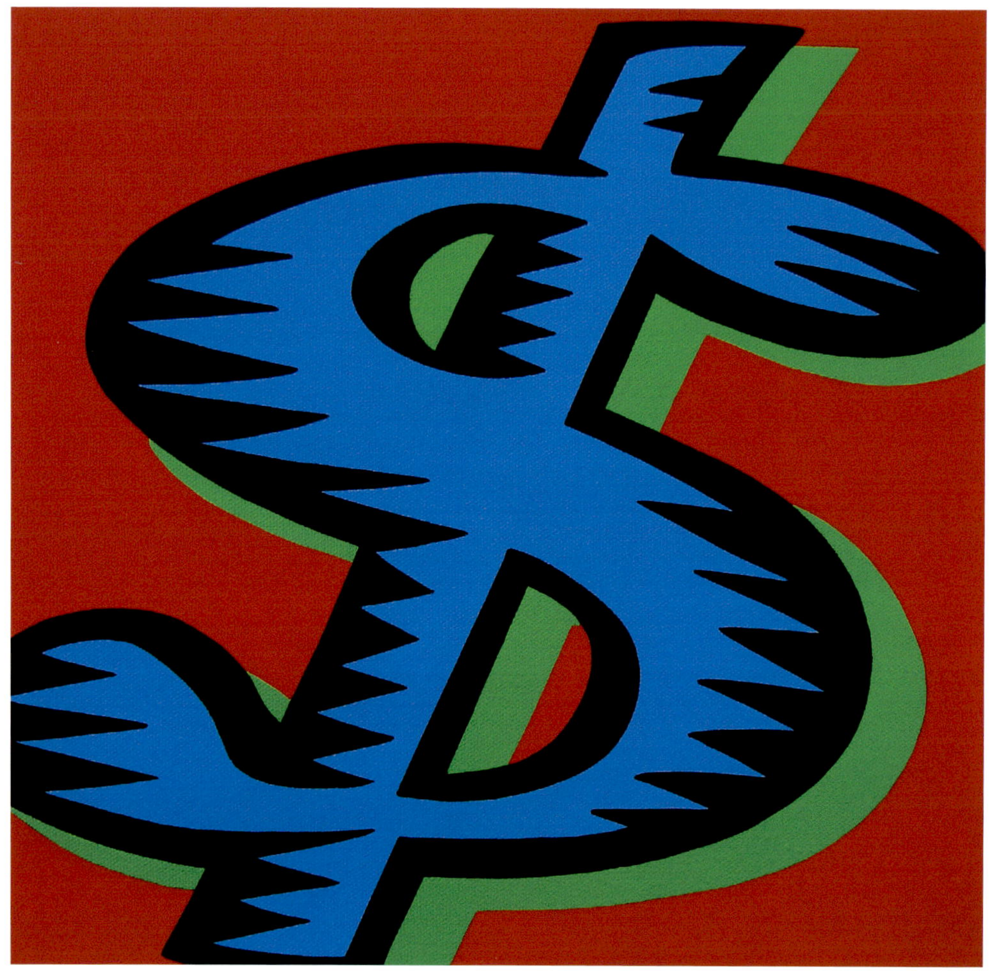

Currency
2007
Acrylic paint on canvas – triptych
12 x 12 x 3 inches
(30.48 x 30.48 x 7.62 cm)

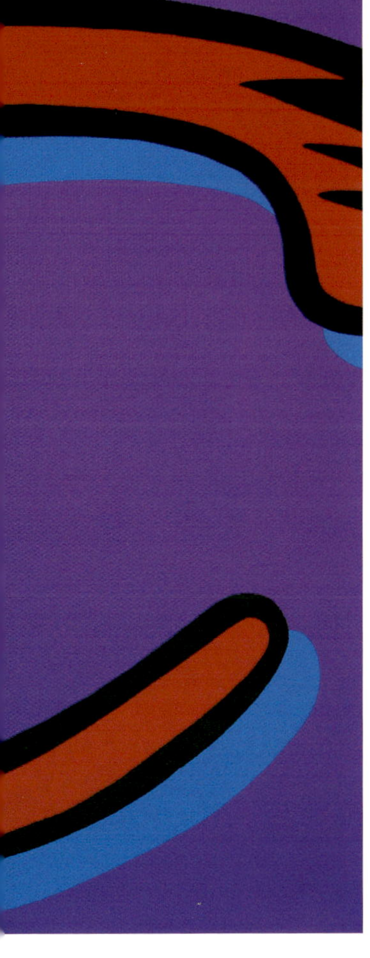
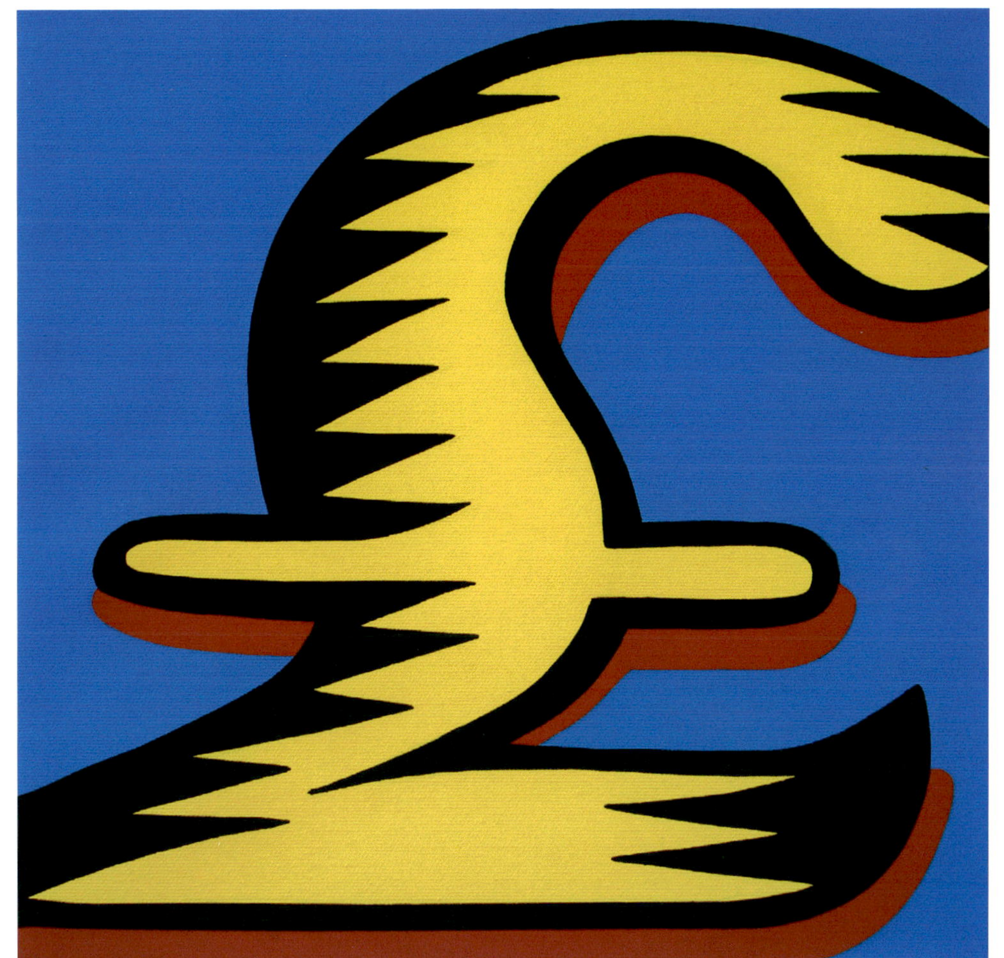

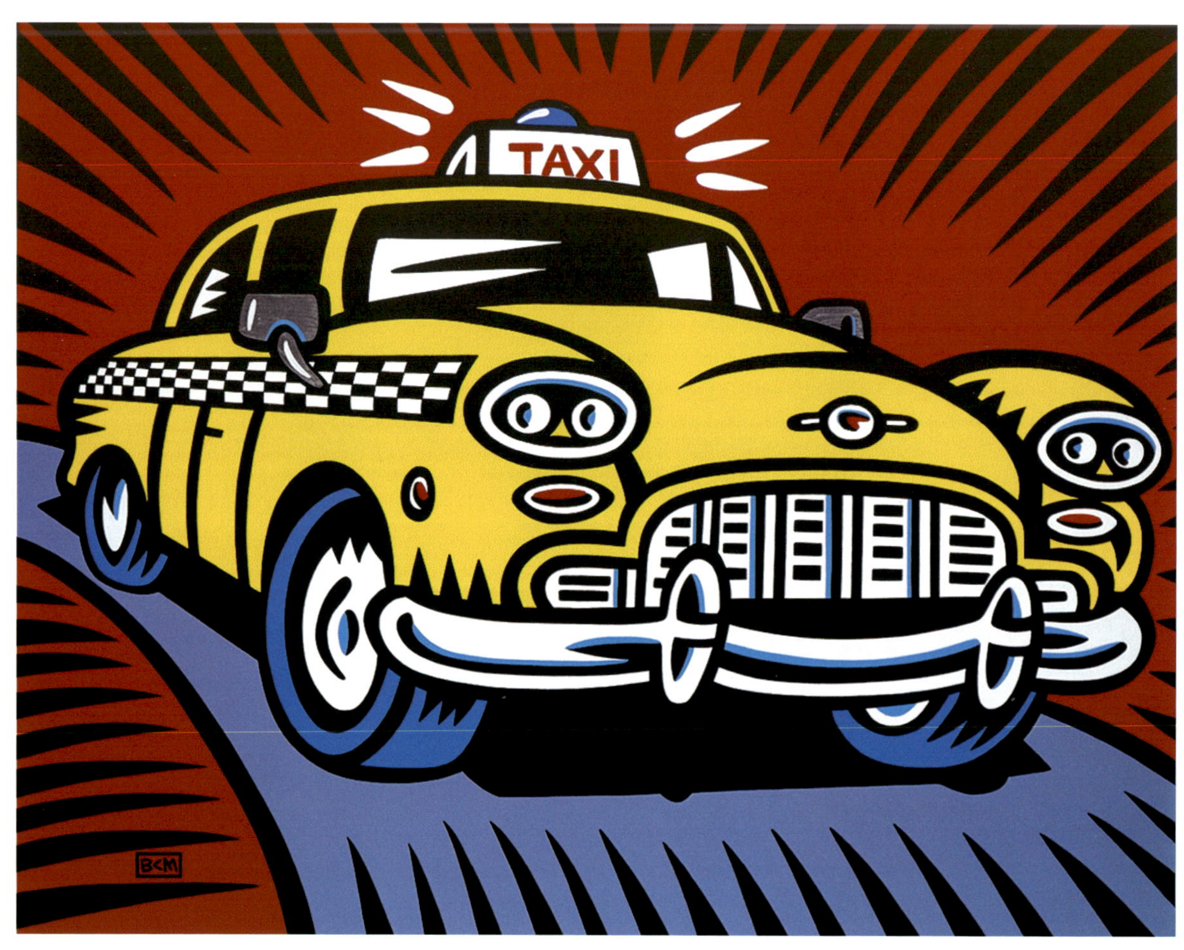

Hey Taxi!
2004
Acrylic paint on canvas
36 x 48 inches
(91.44 x 121.92 cm)

"I love Burton Morris' work!

I love the big bold colors, and the big bold size of his work - and of course I love the wonderful versions of Mickey Mouse he's done - but most of all I really love the big bold IDEAS and insights into character that are such a part of his art. With a few brushstrokes (actually a lot more than a few!) he captures the essence of his subject - and his affection for it - in a way that can't be mistaken for anyone else's.

I love his work!!!"

ROY DISNEY
Director Emeritus
The Walt Disney Corporation

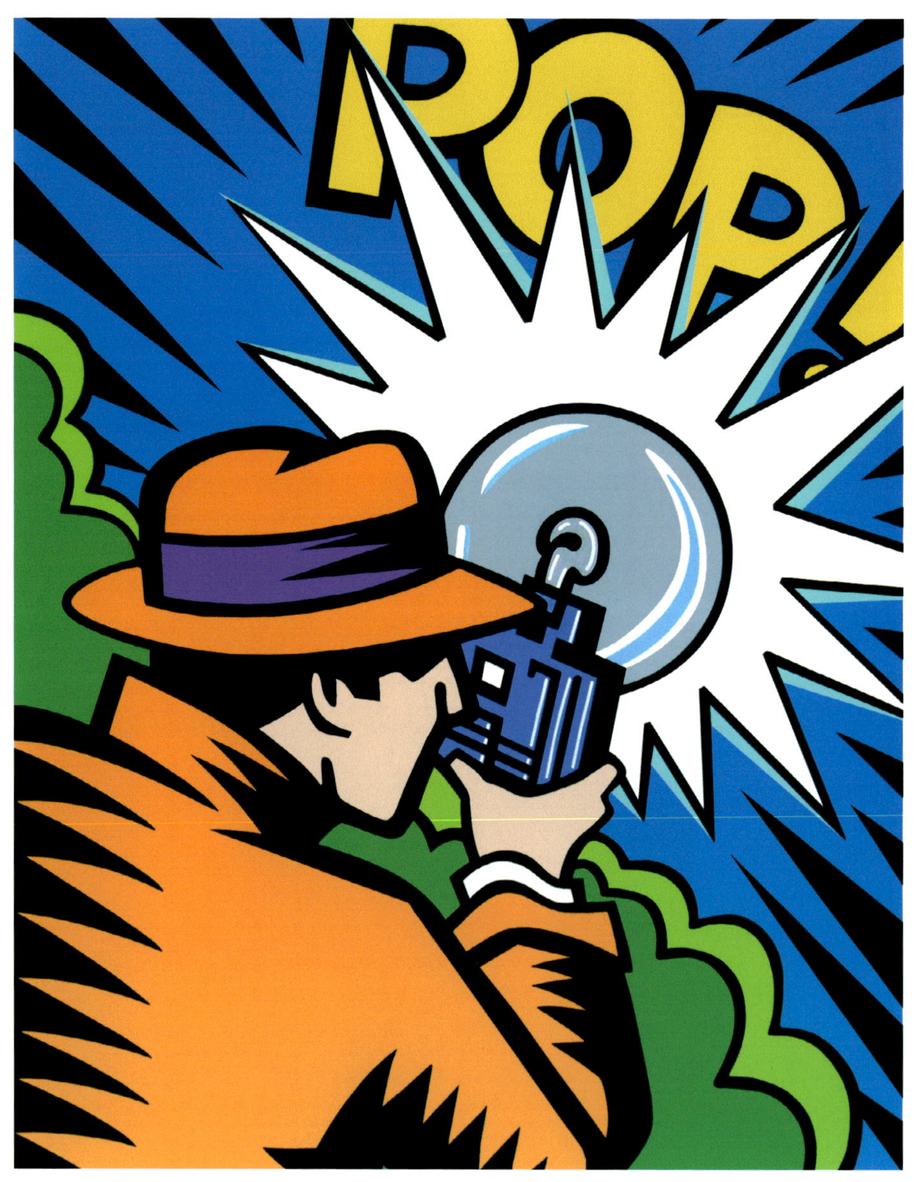

Pop–arazzi A
2007
Acrylic paint on canvas
60 x 48 inches
(152.4 x 121.92 cm)

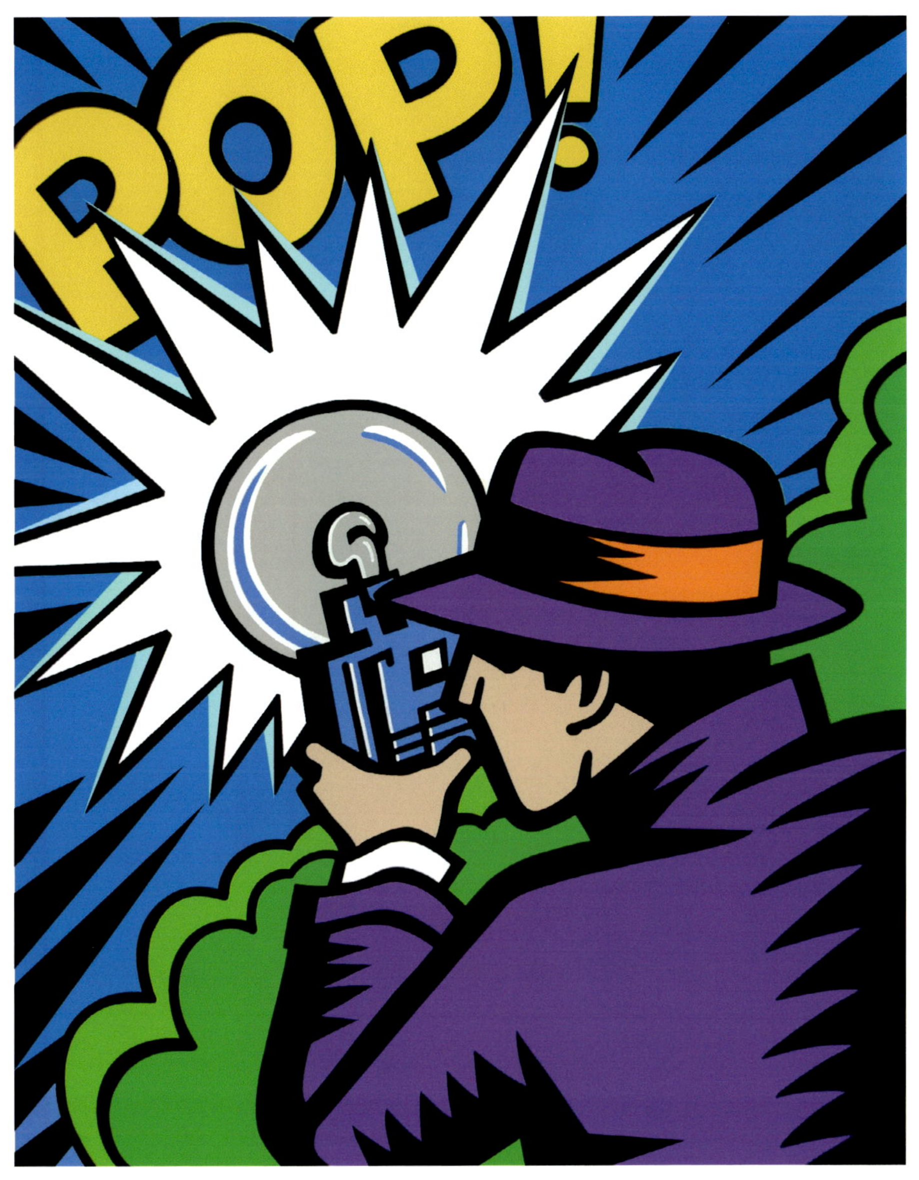

Pop–arazzi B
2007
Acrylic paint on canvas
60 x 48 inches
(152.4 x 121.92 cm)

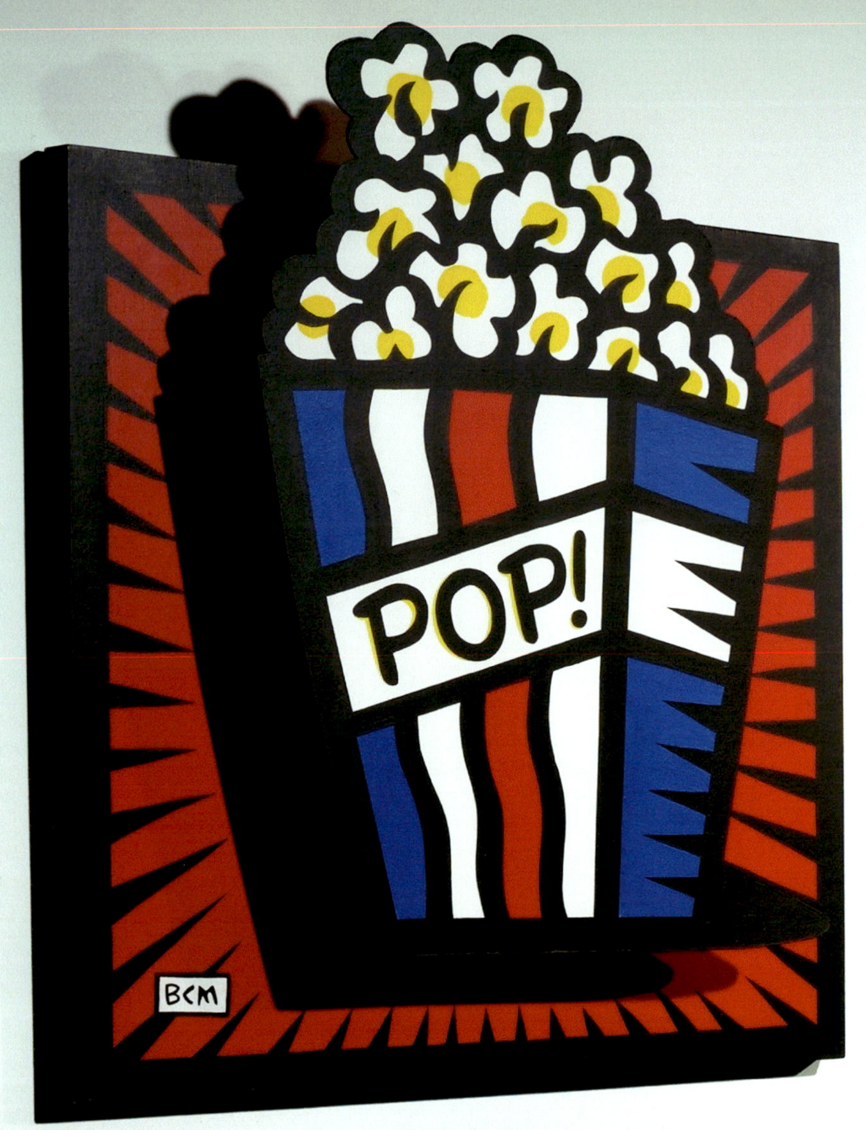
POP!
BCM

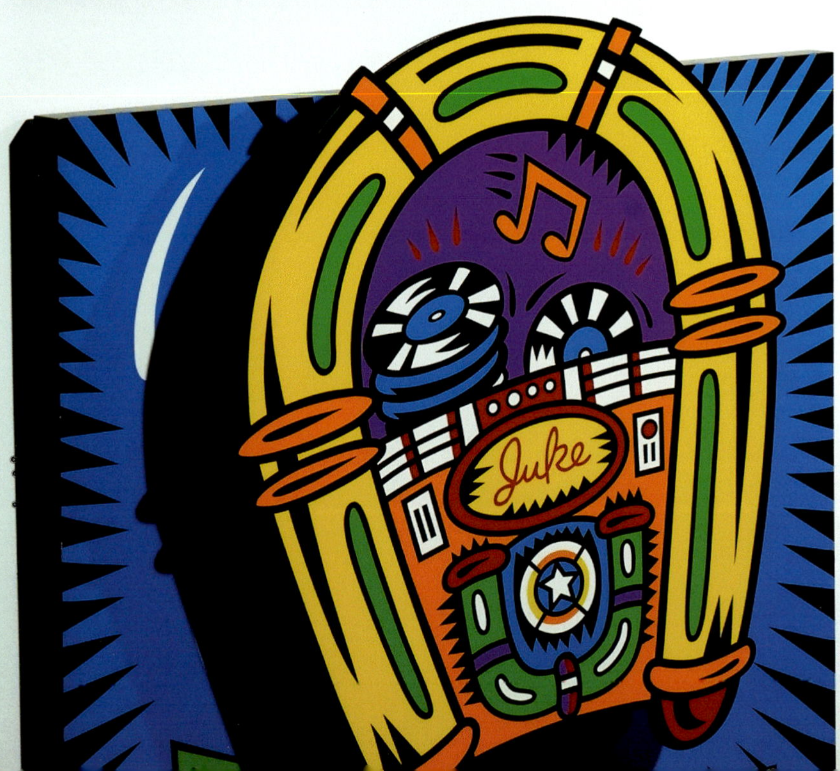
Juke

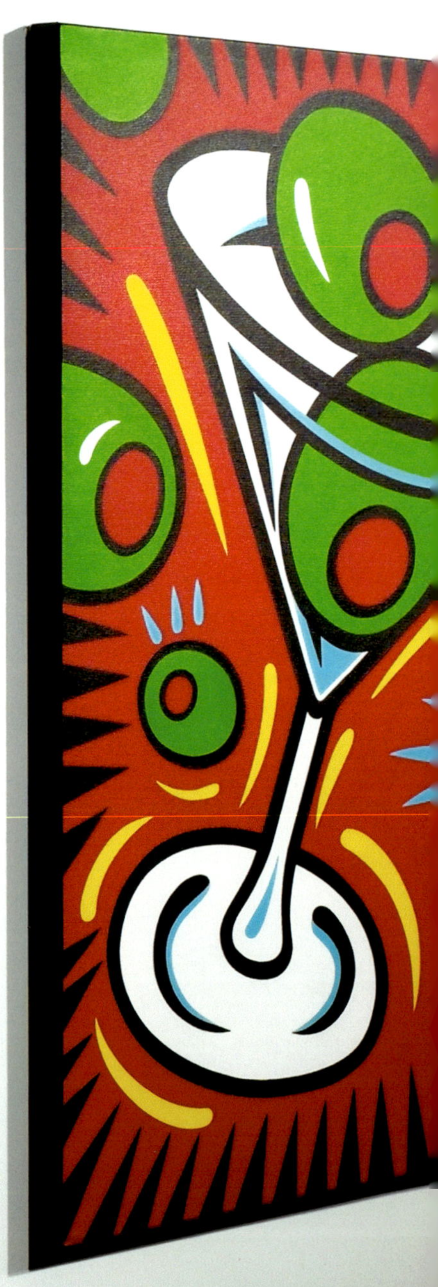

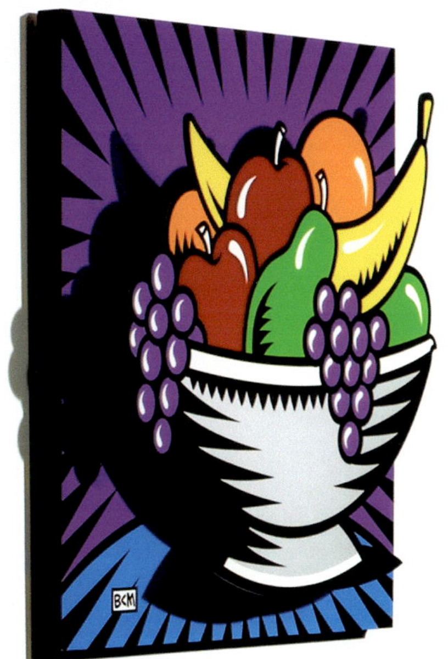
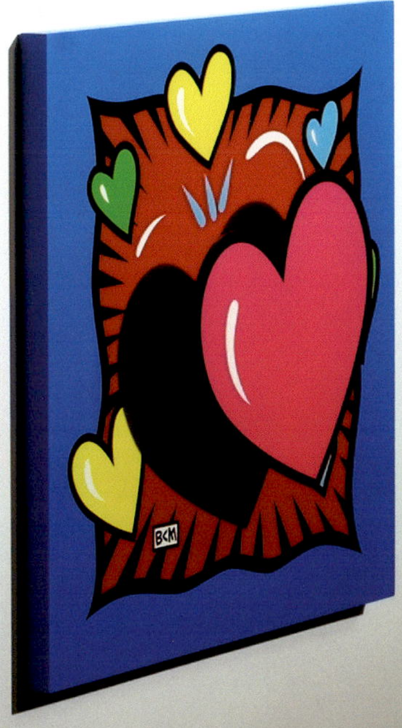
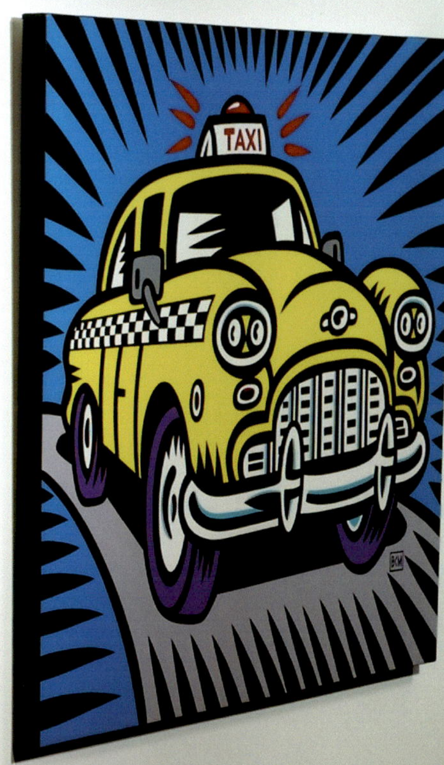

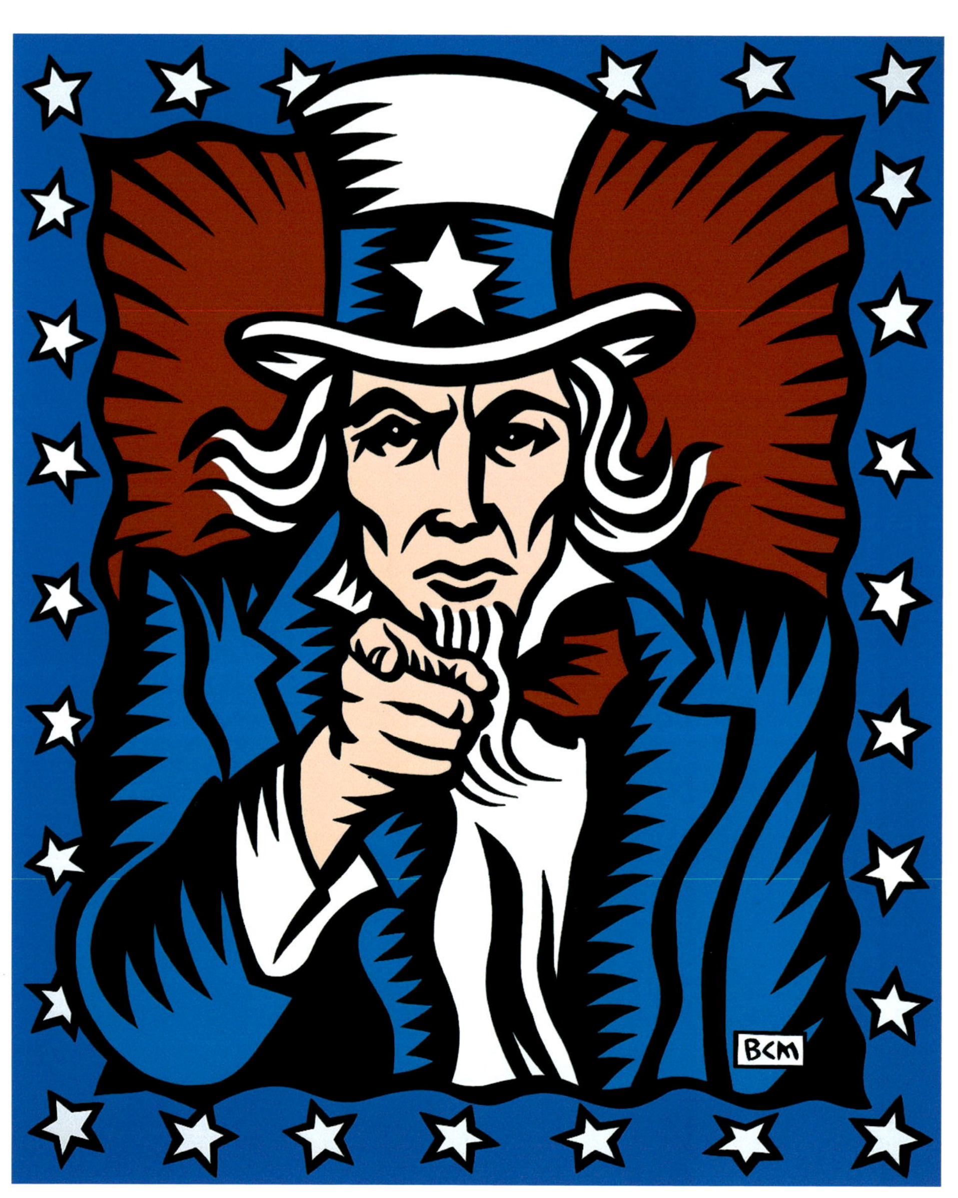

I Want You
1998
Acrylic paint on canvas
48 x 36 inches
(121.92 x 91.44 cm)

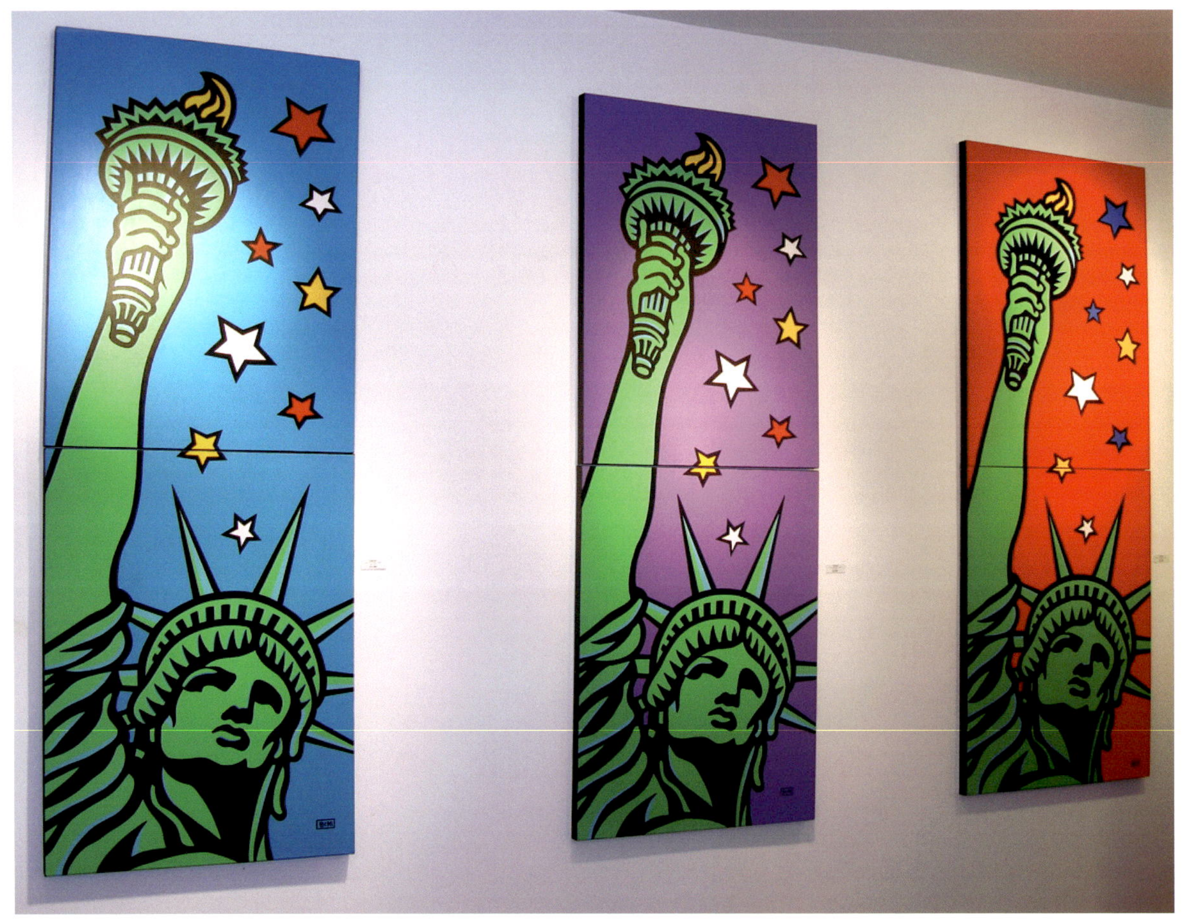

Liberty
2006
Acrylic paint on canvas – triptych
80 x 30 inches
(203.2 x 76.2 cm)

Liberty & Freedom (DETAIL)
2006
Acrylic paint on canvas
30 x 40 inches
(76.2 x 101.6 cm)

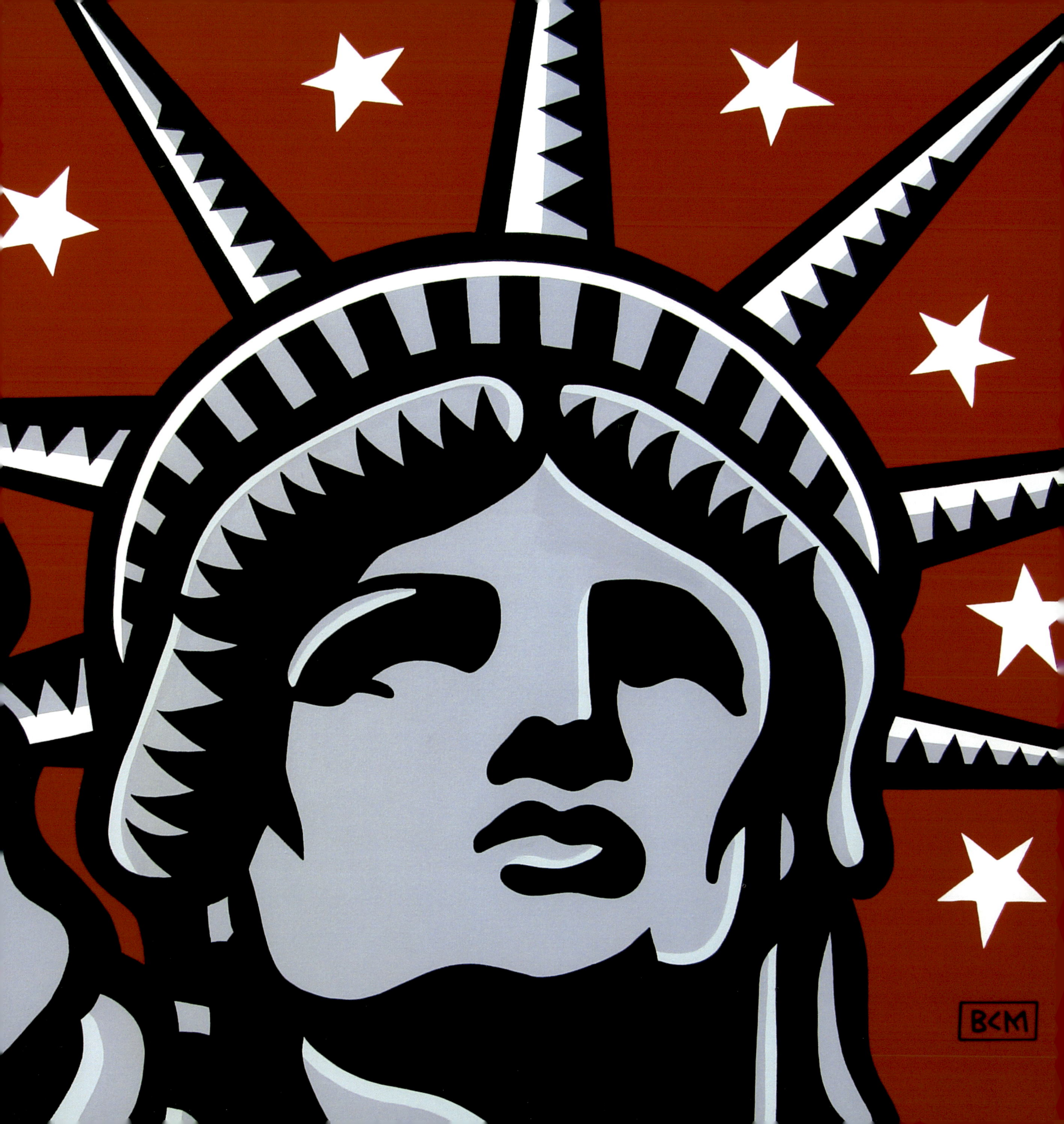

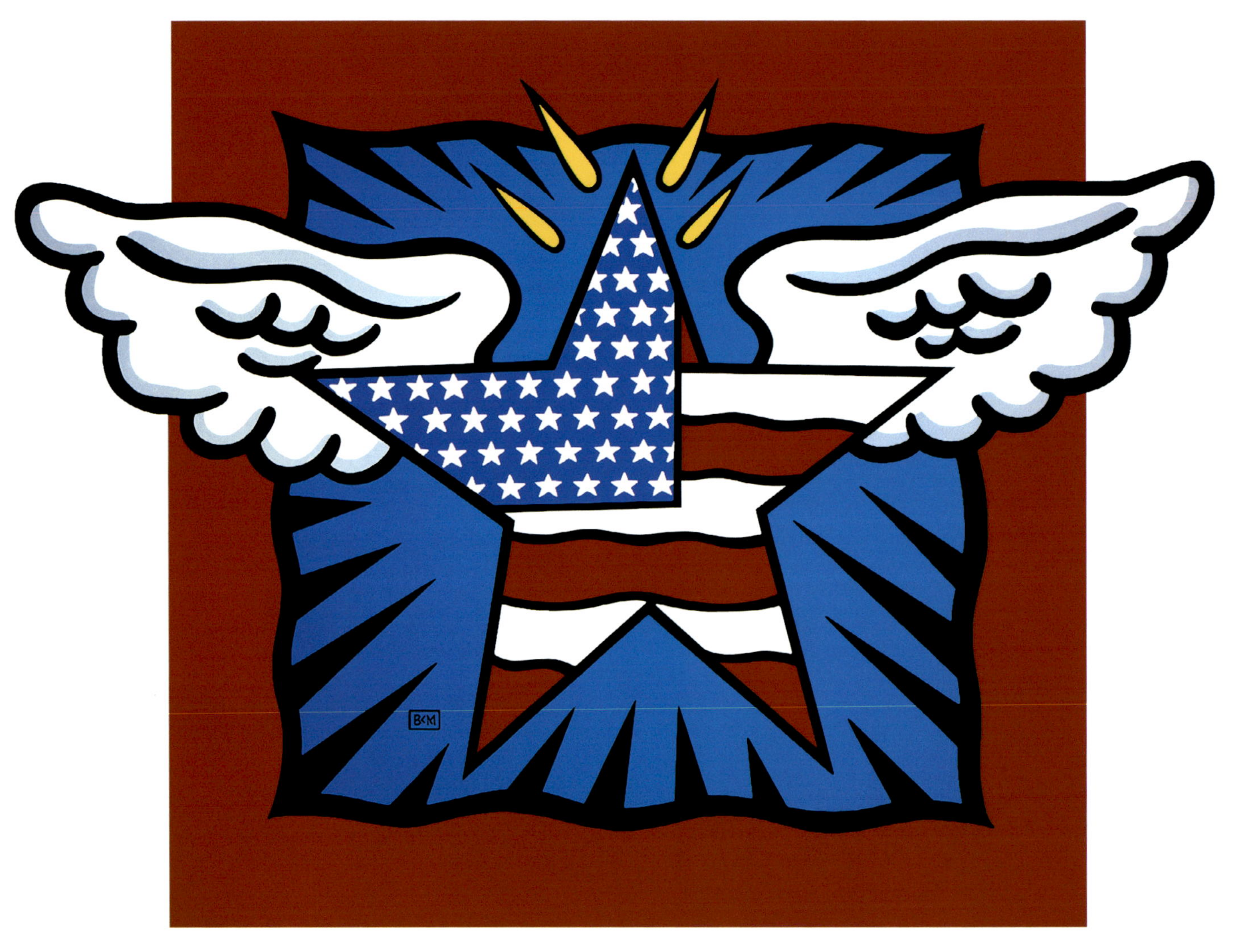

Apprentice Star
2005
Acrylic paint on canvas
with hand cut wood extensions
48 x 48 inches
(121.92 x 121.92 cm)

"Burton Morris' art is everywhere."

DONALD TRUMP
CEO
The Trump Organization*

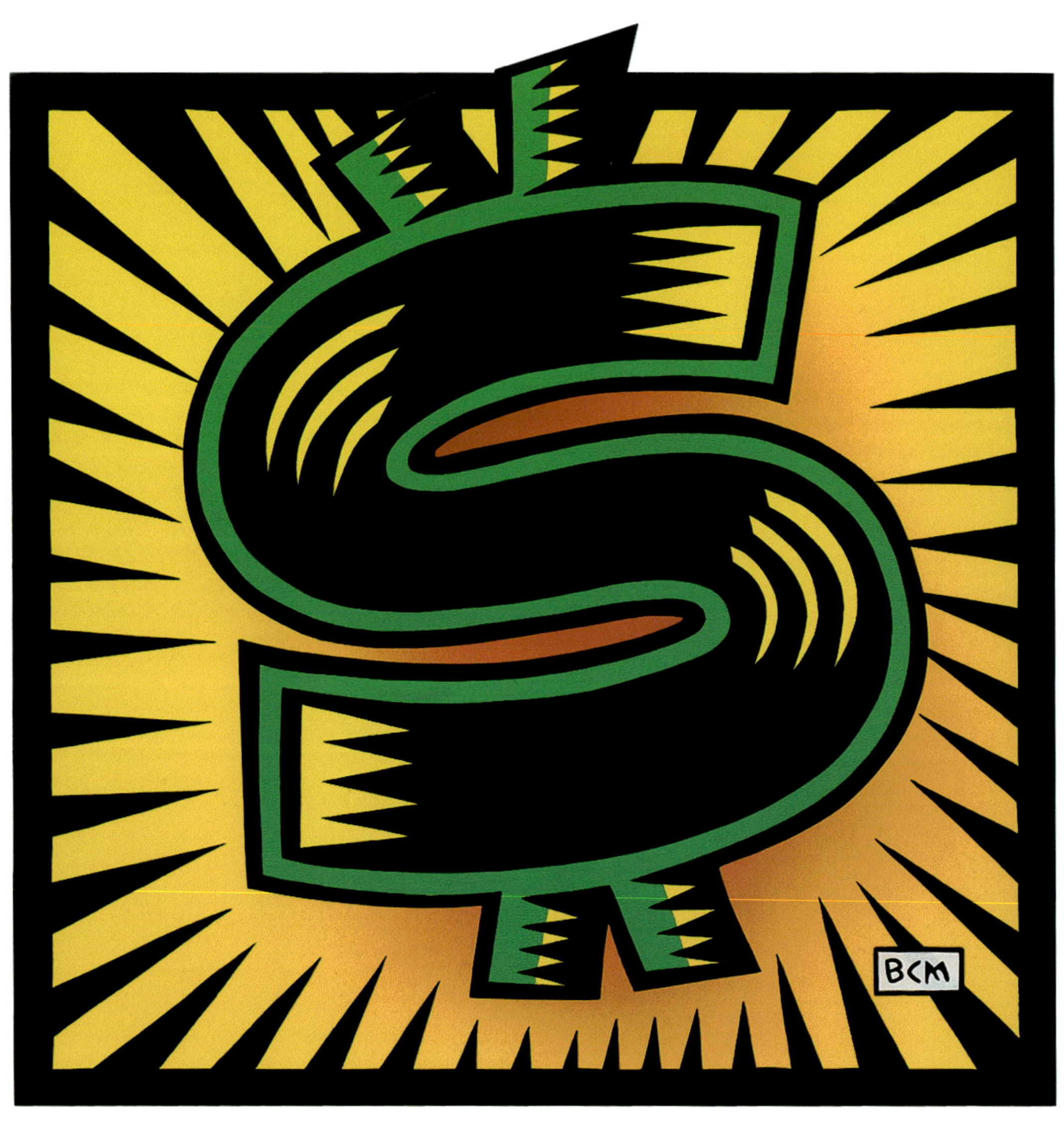

$

2000

Acrylic paint on wood
with wooden dimensional pop-out front panel
24 x 24 x 3 inches
(60.96 x 60.96 x 7.62 cm)

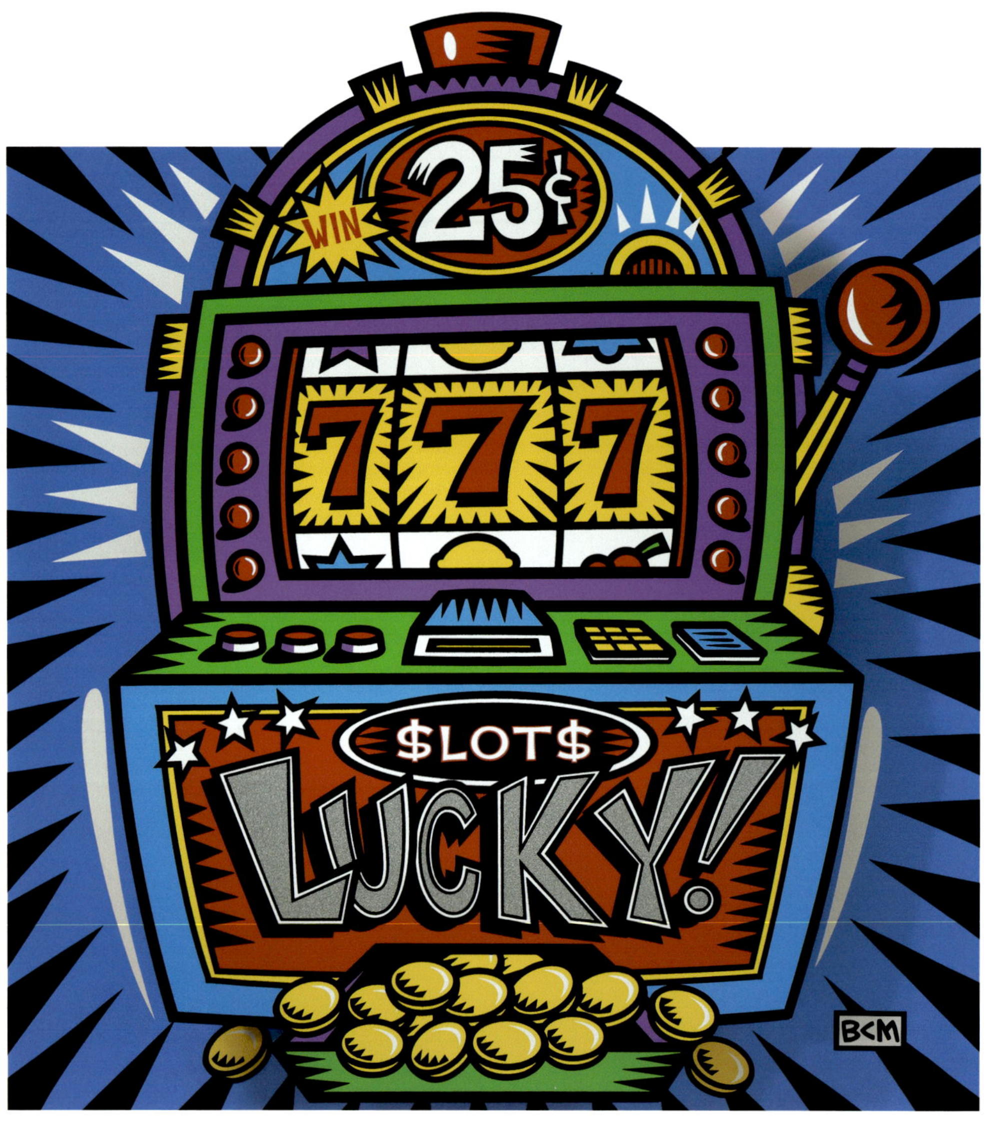
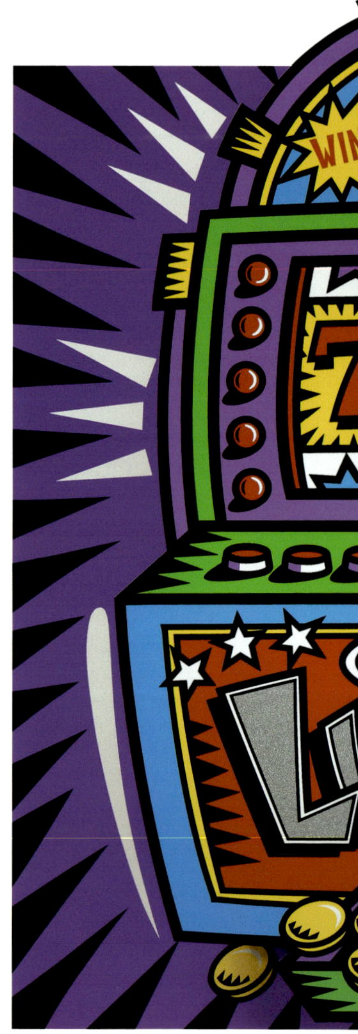

Lucky
2007
Silkscreen ink on gesso board
with dimensional pop–out front panel
Edition of 30
24 x 24 x 3 inches
(60.96 x 60.96 x 10.16 cm)

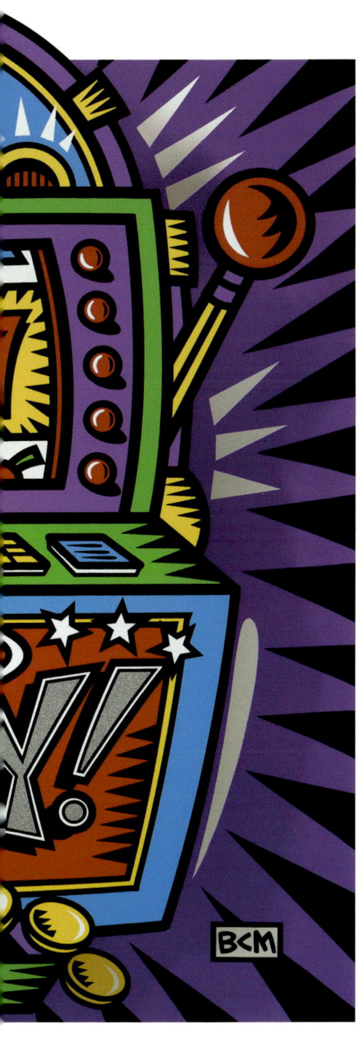
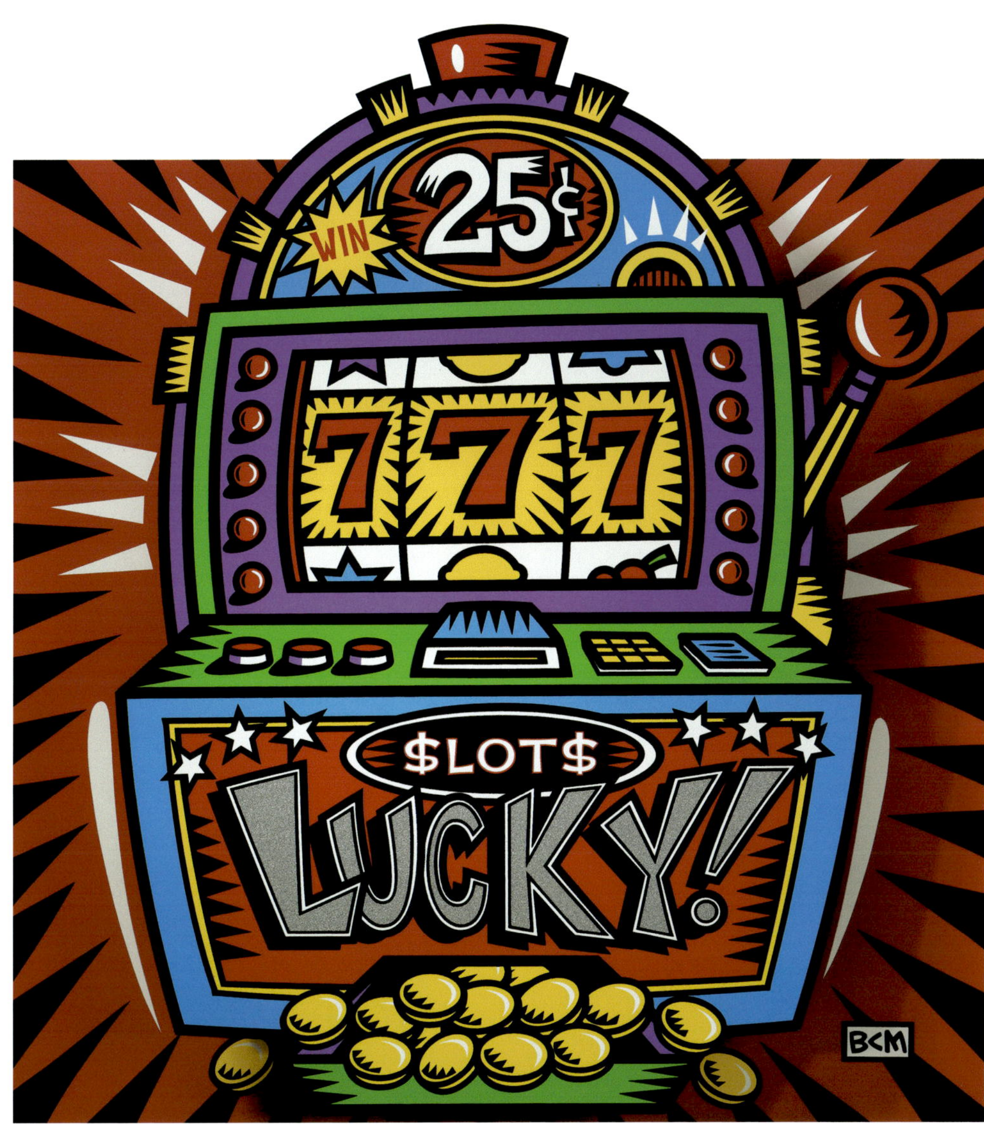
WIN
25¢
777
LOT
LUCKY!
BCM

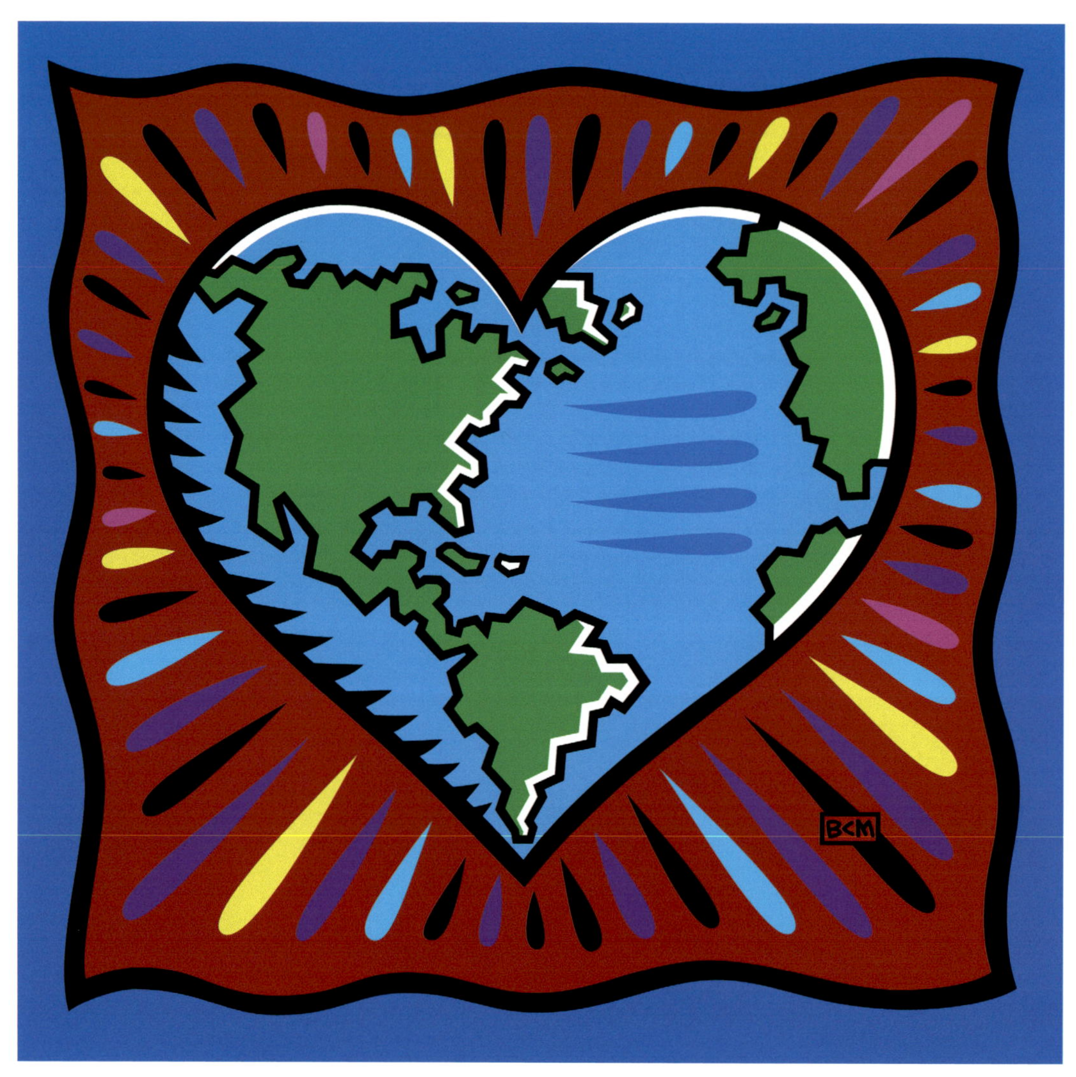

Earth Heart
2005
Acrylic paint on canvas
54 x 54 inches
(137.16 x 137.16 cm)

"Earth Heart represents much more than
Burton's extraordinary talent. It literally represents
the size of his heart.

Through his contribution as commemorative artist
for our foundation's 10th Grand Slam for
Children event, he enabled us to touch the lives
of hundreds of children in Las Vegas.

I am grateful for his generosity and friendship."

ANDRE AGASSI
Tennis Legend

American Dog
1996
Acrylic paint on canvas
48 x 60 inches
(121.92 x 152.4 cm)

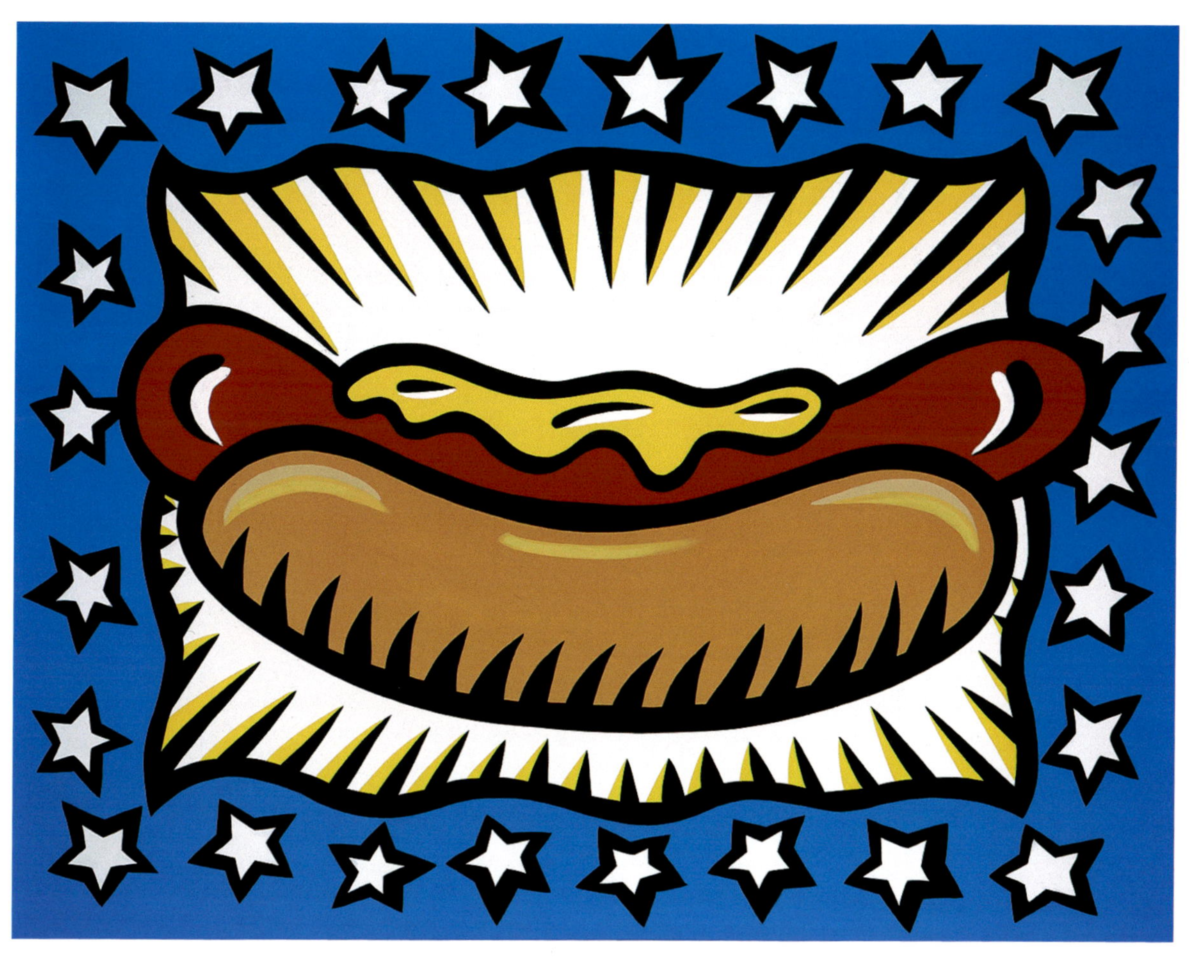

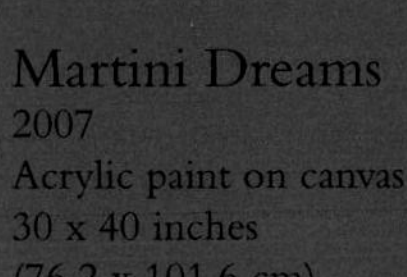

Martini Dreams
2007
Acrylic paint on canvas
30 x 40 inches
(76.2 x 101.6 cm)

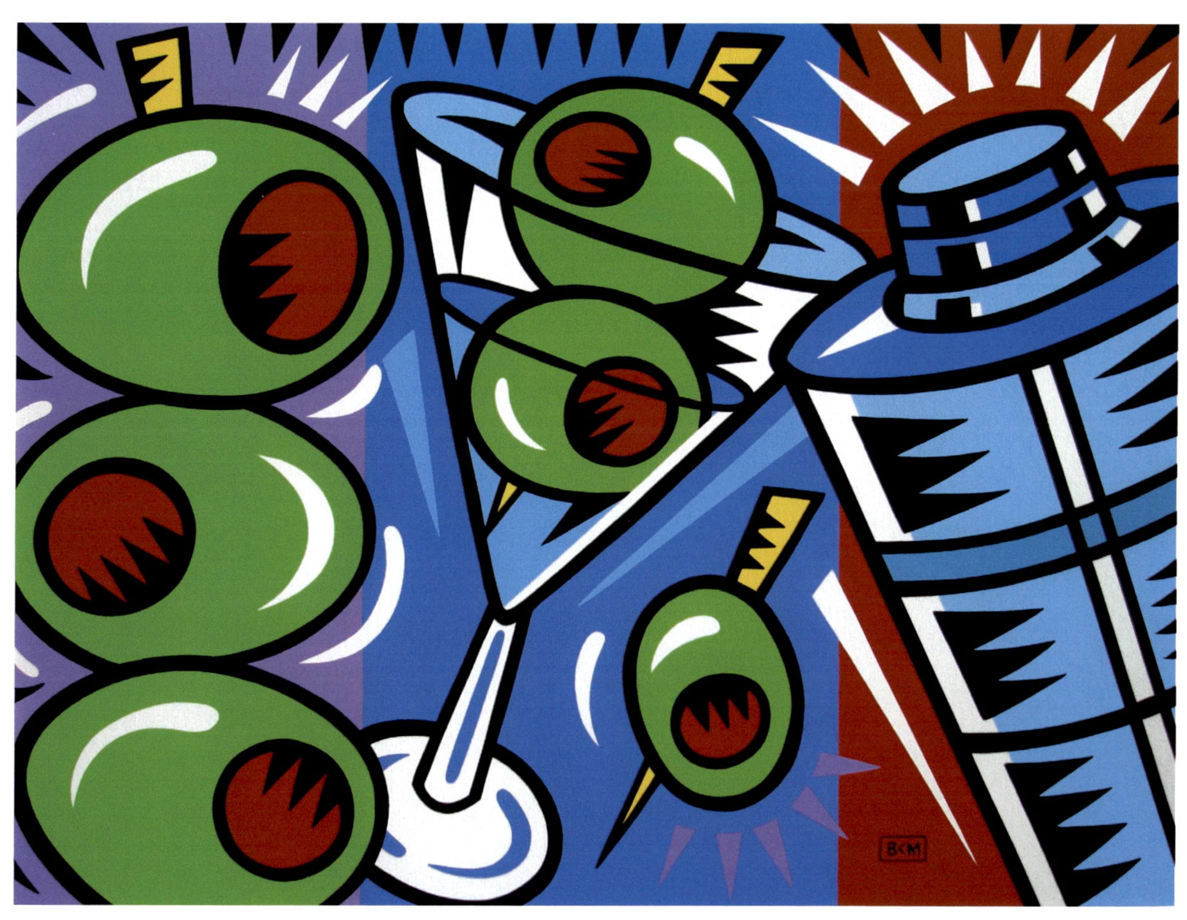

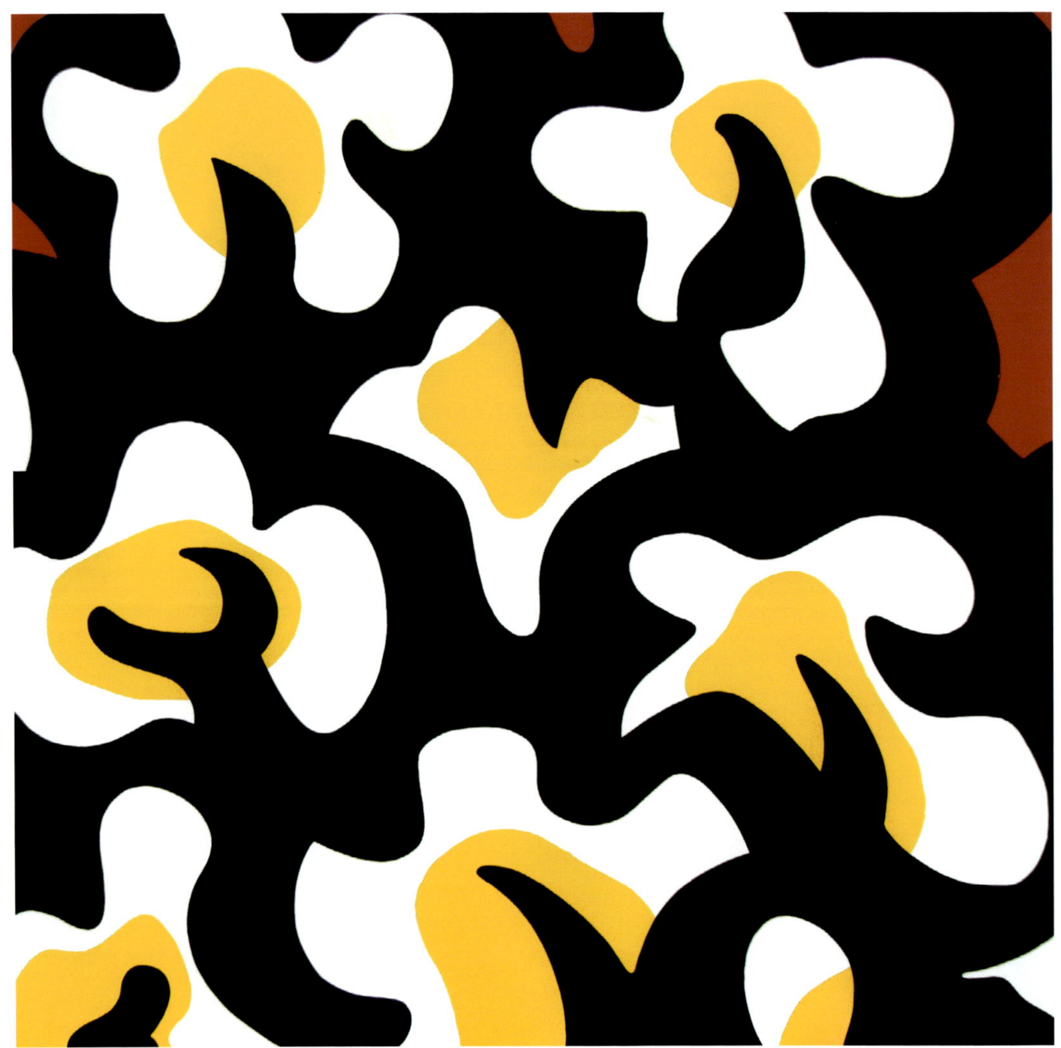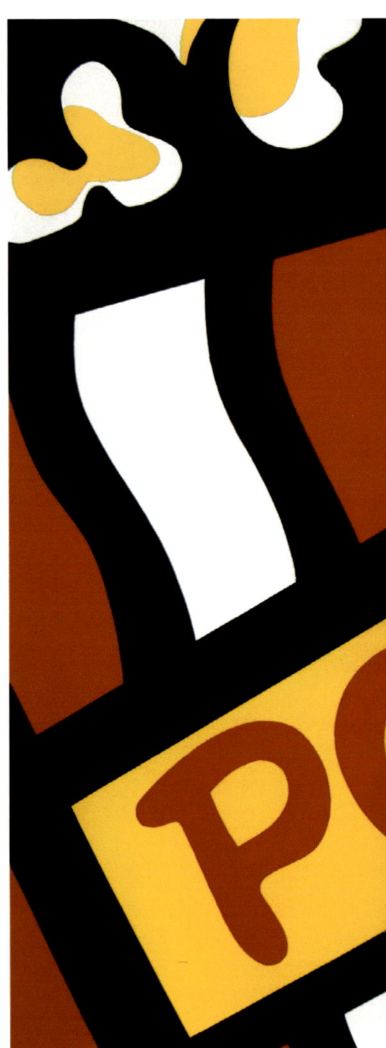

Kernels and Pop!
2007
Acrylic paint on canvas – triptych
24 x 24 inches each
(60.96 x 60.96 cm)

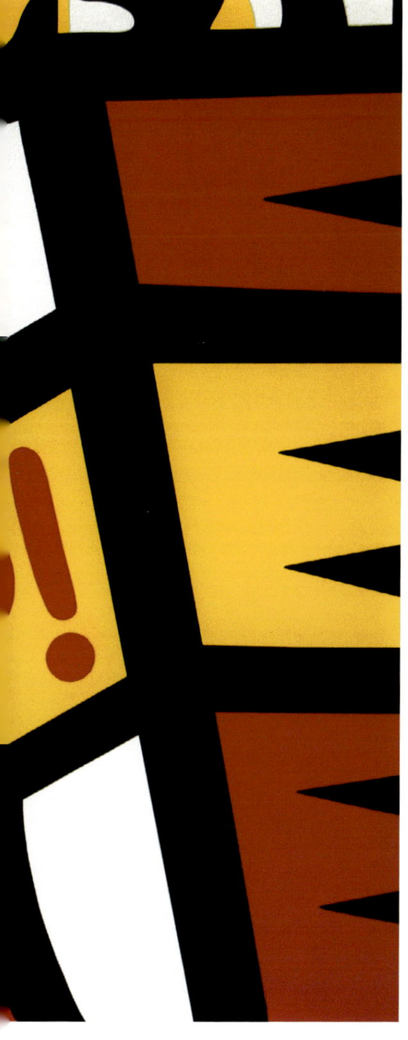

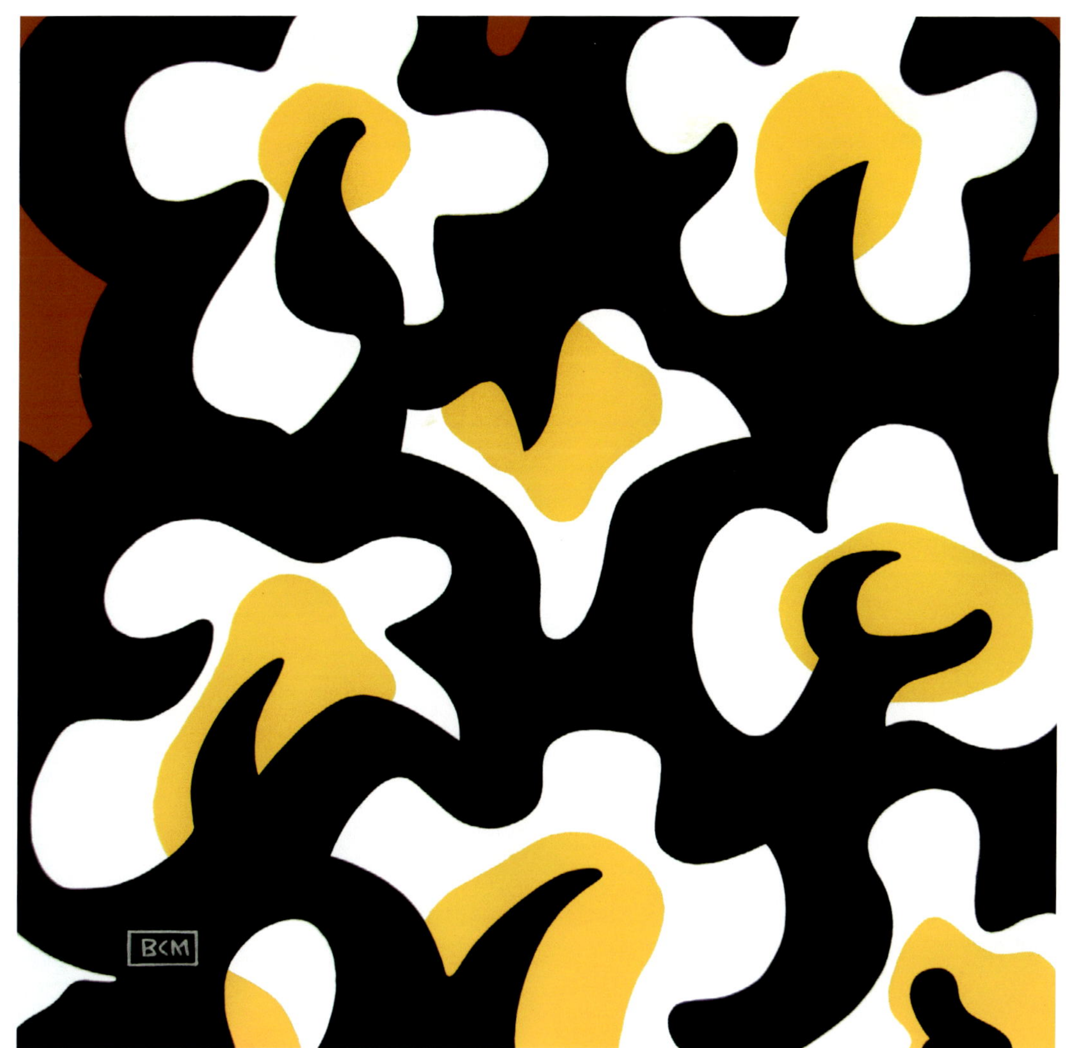
BCM